This book is dedicated to my adoring husband Bobby, who gives me far more love than disasters. With him I will live happily ever after.

To Write the Author

If you wish to contact the author or would like more information about this book, please write to the author in care of Llewellyn Worldwide, and we will forward your request. Both the author and publisher appreciate hearing from you and learning of your enjoyment of this book and how it has helped you. Llewellyn Worldwide cannot guarantee that every letter written to the author can be answered, but all will be forwarded. Please write to:

Tiffany Johnson
℅ Llewellyn Worldwide
2143 Wooddale Drive
Woodbury, MN 55125-2989

Please enclose a self-addressed stamped envelope for reply, or $1.00 to cover costs. If outside the USA, enclose an international postal reply coupon.

FIND YOUR HAPPILY *Ever After*

Love and Relationship Advice From a Professional Psychic

TIFFANY JOHNSON

Llewellyn Publications
Woodbury, Minnesota

FIRST EDITION
First Printing, 2015

Book design by Bob Gaul
Cover design by Ellen Lawson
Cover image: iStockphoto.com/14300813/©Talaj,
iStockphoto.com/19247116/©Дмитрий Грибов
Editing by Ed Day
Part Page Art by Llewellyn Art Department

Library of Congress Cataloging-in-Publication Data
Johnson, Tiffany.
Find your happily ever after: love and relationship advice from a professional psychic/Tiffany Johnson.—First Edition.
pages cm
ISBN 978-0-7387-4192-5
1. Occultism. 2. Sex—Miscellanea. 3. Love—Miscellanea. 4. Interpersonal relations—Miscellanea. I. Title.
BF1442.S53J64 2015
131—dc23
2014040978

Llewellyn Publications
A Division of Llewellyn Worldwide Ltd.
2143 Wooddale Drive
Woodbury, MN 55125-2989
www.llewellyn.com
Printed in the United States of America

Contents

Foreword by Cooper Lawrence *xi*

Introduction *1*

Part One: Things You Need to Know Before Diving In

One: In the Beginning 7

Two: Soul Mates 11

Three: Settling Versus the One 19

Four: Deal Breakers 25

Five: The Dork Within 37

Six: They Don't Care What You Wear or What You Drive 43

Seven: The Most Important Attributes 49

Eight: Bad Boys and Girls 55

Nine: Change 63

Ten: If You're Not Feeling It in the First Five Dates 73

Part Two: You've Made It Past Five Dates, Now What?

Eleven: Commitment-Phobia 81

Twelve: Make Each Other Better 85

Thirteen: Romance, People! 93

Fourteen: Moving In Together 101

Fifteen: Privacy 109

Sixteen: Me Time 115

Seventeen: Long-Distance Relationships 123

Eighteen: Love Isn't All You Need 131

Nineteen: If You Think They Are Cheating 139

Twenty: Abusive Relationships 149

Part Three: Take Stock, Learn, Move On, and Try Again

Twenty-One: Blame Is for Suckers 161

Twenty-Two: Letting Go 165

Twenty-Three: After the Breakup 175

Twenty-Four: Karma and Past Lives 183

Twenty-Five: What the Other Side Thinks about Love 193

Twenty-Six: My Mama Told Me 199

Twenty-Seven: Take Your Own Advice 205

Twenty-Eight: Do You Need a Psychic or Common Sense? 213

Conclusion 217

Acknowledgments 221

About the Author 223

Foreword

A psychic medium writing a book on relationships? Why not? Tiffany is as knowledgeable as any expert in the field; even without the fancy letters after her name, she is the voice of authority.

Her advice is no-nonsense and to the point. She gives people what they are looking for: answers! She also provides very effective techniques and most importantly, things to think about in their personal relationships.

More than just a relationship book, *Find Your Happily Ever After: Love and Relationship Advice From a Professional Psychic* is a book to better yourself, therein, making your relationships work better for you.

Most importantly, Tiffany covers the psychic-y stuff, this is what makes her so unique. She gives you the 411 on everything from what soul mates are (and what they aren't) to the role of karma in a relationship.

Whether or not you believe in psychics is irrelevant. *Find Your Happily Ever After* is about something we all want—bettering our romantic relationships. What you'll find most is that Tiffany knows about love and is willing to share her insight. She lets you in on the real deal about dating and love and doesn't sugarcoat much. It's an incredibly honest approach. The bonus is that as a psychic, you get to learn from her about the deeper, soulful, meaningful connections that will only help you be happier.

—Cooper Lawrence, author of *The Yoga Club*

Introduction

By no means am I a relationship expert. I don't have any fancy letters after my name. I don't have any advanced degrees designating anything to acknowledge my end all-be all familiarity in romantic endeavors like Dr. Phil and Dr. Laura (or any other alleged love guru), but that isn't going to stop me from trying to help you out.

What I do have in my intellectual arsenal is over two decades of speaking with people about their relationships. Most of those conversations are about romantic relationships. So, I think that gives me some insight into how they may work, and, frankly, how, sometimes, they don't. That is always unfortunate, but it is the reality of today's world.

I am, by profession, a psychic and medium. About 80 percent of my daily readings focus on relationships. This includes familial relationships, friendships, and workplace connections, but most of my time is focused solely on romantic relationships—in the crush form, dating, exclusive relationships, friends with benefits, on the outs...I could go on and on. Love does, indeed, make the world go 'round. But goodness knows that love doesn't make things simple; hence, the questions that are presented to me during my day-to-day readings.

At least once a day, a client will say "I know you must get sick of this," or "you must hear this all the time, but..." followed by the individual asking about their particular romantic issue. I'm quick to answer that no, I absolutely do not get sick of tuning in (you'll see me use that term quite frequently regarding my use of psychic abilities) to an individual's relationships.

The first thing I do when tuning in to someone's relationship is ask for the name of the person my client has questions about. From there, what comes through is that person's attitude, their motivations, their character, and their perceptions about the relationship. I then relay that information to the client who in turn gives confirmation. Getting the other person's perspective gives me far more information than the client is usually willing to provide. Being able to hear one side of the story (from my client) and having the ability to see the other, paints a perfectly clear picture and explains the behavior of both parties. It enlightens me to the cause and effect. By knowing what both parties want, I can provide my client clear guidance and direction. Sadly, sometimes that guidance is a suggestion to end the relationship altogether.

I'm really happy to help and shed some insight where I can. I am human after all. I've dated. I've had the intense crush. I've had my heart broken. I have had to end relationships when I saw they weren't beneficial. And now, for almost (at the time I'm writing this) twenty years, I've been married. So, I get it.

What you will get out of this book is the reality of relationships. Not the psychology behind it, but the reality of truth and dating and romance.

So I hope, dear reader, you're getting the gist. Although I have had the grand opportunity and honor to speak with thousands of folks all over the world throughout the years via psychic readings, I by no means am without experience and personal life lessons. I've walked the walk, enjoyed the blessed moments, and certainly wallowed in the tough ones. Hopefully, combining all of what I've learned, heard, and experienced, I can share just a little wisdom with you, as you walk on your relationship path.

Part One

Things You Need to Know Before Diving In

One

In the Beginning

I've been providing readings for over twenty years. I know it may sound a little weird, but I started reading for people at my mom's kitchen table when I was just a child. In fact, one of my very first readings was for my mom. It gave me a lot of insight into her relationship (she was divorced by the time we did the reading) with my biological father. To her, it was just confirmation of what she already knew and understood. But I think on some level, it validated her feelings and actions that she had taken, letting go of the relationship years prior.

I grew up having psychic experiences my entire life. Many of my earliest memories are having late-night visits from souls on the other side. To me, it was just normal—and when you're about three years old, you just go with it. They were very transparent, shadowy figures that would be in the room, chatting away, and I would listen to what they had to say, report it to my mom the next morning, and then go watch *Sesame Street.* Just another day in the life of a young, up-and-coming psychic.

I was raised in a fairly normal household, although my parents divorced when I was five years old. Believe it or not, divorce was still a little out of the ordinary back in the 1970s. That was the only thing that really stood out about my childhood, outside of the psychic thing, of course. However, the divorce did play a part. At a fairly young age, I heard and saw, firsthand, how relationships fell apart. So, just because I perceive myself to be a romantic doesn't mean that I don't have a sound grasp of reality regarding those partnerships. That also doesn't mean I haven't gotten hurt, because I have on numerous occasions.

From there, I grew up and dealt with my own up-and-down, topsy-turvy relationships. It was pretty evident, at least to me, that I was completely into the whole love game early on. And I'm proud to say that I still keep in contact with a very serious boyfriend from third grade. (Sarcasm). All joking aside, he's a wonderful photographer and has done several press/PR shots for me. I started dating around the age of sixteen and had my first serious boyfriend in my junior year of high school. We dated a year and things ended when he enlisted in the Marine Corps. And yes, during those hormone-laden years, I was providing readings outside class time as well.

I had a couple serious relationships in my late teens and early twenties, but I fell madly and deeply in love when I met Bobby. We met at a bar. How romantic is that? He was out with his girlfriend and Nick, his best friend, who was also his roommate. I was out with a bunch of my guy friends when I saw Nick's beautiful hair and struck up a conversation. I started dating Nick, and when he brought me over to his house, there sat Bobby on the couch. One evening when it was just the two of us, Bobby and I started talking—and talking—until I finally fell asleep on the couch at two in the morning. Nick was surprised that Bobby and I hit it off so well because Bobby didn't like anybody, but we instantly had a deep connection, and we eloped four months later. Would I recommend this path for everyone? Heck no. In fact, I'd advise against it. It wasn't easy. (Think about it—we really only got to know one another because I was dating his closest friend. That's a whole other story that's rife with conflicting emotion and turmoil for all three of us. Reconciliation did occur...eventually.) And Bobby and I had to reconcile our experience gap. My husband had been married before and I was only twenty-one. Enough said. So we both had baggage, although mine was brand-new and his was a little banged up and torn. And both of us were chock-full of issues, the big ones being youth (me) and trust (him). Needless to say, within one year of marriage, we went right from blissful new love to marriage counseling. We were not about to give up easily, and I am proud to say that we made it through despite the odds (age, trust, families). Although no relationship is ever perfect, I'm not only a happy girl, but I understand how lucky I am.

Two

Soul Mates

Oh the question of soul mates, I hear it almost every day. As the old saying goes, if I had a dime for every time . . . Well, maybe in this economy I would need a quarter. Regardless, it's a big topic of conversation in my day-to-day readings. But I get it. We're all looking for that special someone. Some of us seem to have found the One and others find that area a bit more challenging. Let's talk about what soul mates really are, the expectations, and, most importantly, the reality.

I blame dating website commercials for the overuse of the term "soul mates." I get the marketing technique, but why do they need to oversensationalize? Of course—that's the whole ad game, right? I've gotten up on countless soapboxes professing my contempt with their romanticizing of the term. Unfortunately, it portrays the wrong premise. It gives folks the idea that A: finding your soul mate is the end all-be all and that B: soul mates are purely romantic in nature. Both of which aren't necessarily true.

I asked people for definitions of "soul mates" on my social media pages (I love using them for informal focus groups), and I got varied responses. Before we go any further, I should probably share my thoughts and viewpoints so you can understand where I'm coming from.

I believe that we, in fact, do have soul mates. However, my perception isn't what some would probably consider traditional. First, I do not believe that they are necessarily romantic in nature. Shocking, right? I believe that our soul mate may be a platonic friend. Like a best friend. Your soul mate may be your mom or dad! Can it be a romantic partner? Sure. But, over the course of twenty years in personal private readings, I've maybe seen that less than a couple dozen times.

We learn and grow from everyone we encounter. However, with our soul mates, it's a deeper connection and communication—that has nothing to do with romantic attraction. Our soul mates are here to help our souls evolve. That's a pretty daunting task. And, although nifty, soul evolution has nothing to do with physical intimacy. One last thing to consider is that if we were all with our soul mate (and it's a romantic partner), we would all be in bed all the time and nothing would get accomplished. Well maybe not nothing.

Can we have romantic relationships with our soul mate? Sure. All things are possible in the spiritual world. As I mentioned, however, connecting in a romantic way with your soul mate is a pretty rare occurrence. Although we learn magical, wonderful things from our partners in life, oftentimes it's more about weathering the challenges with them than that absolute, soulful connection. Just because someone isn't your designated soul mate doesn't mean that relationship is any less significant! That'd be pretty shallow of the Universe!

Let's jump into reality for a moment. We, having the human existence, typically learn a lot more from our bad experiences than we learn from the good. It's not fun, and sometimes it's an out-and-out bummer, but it's true. Things we don't like or care for take up a lot more room in our head than those that we enjoy. Part of that is simply survival instinct. Without it we'd continually burn ourselves or eat poisonous things. Beyond just basic survival, we learn patience by feeling impatient. We learn to control our temper by getting angry. See where I'm going here, folks? Life is, and I've said it many times before and look for it to be repeated soon, about the experience. And experience, by its nature is as good as it is bad. So, having that perfect romantic relationship may not be all it's cracked up to be!

Quite a few folks have asked the question, "Can we have more than one soul mate?" As the term "mate" is singular, it's a pretty good question to ask. Honestly, I'm unsure. My gut tells me that it is a one-and-only type of thing. I don't think you can have many. However, the term soul group consists of various souls making up a unit with a singular bond/directive. I think that these groups have a collective unconscious that drives them not only to one another, but to a unified goal. Ultimately, the goal is most important, but they work best together. When working as a team and having that connectedness, there is a deeper connection than focusing energies with other random individuals.

Soul groups originate on the other side. The idea is that as a group, the lesson can be not only learned as a unit, but brought forth in a more efficient manner by the group. The idea of a soul group is not for everyone to get along in this lifetime. That's wonderful if that's the case, but sometimes, it's not. We often use difficulty or adversity to grow beyond what we perceive as our limitations. So—although unpleasant, a member of a soul group may not be your best friend.

An example of a soul group is the collective of survivors from 9/11. These people went through a horrific experience together. Some were at Ground Zero during the massive event. Some were not there in person but had lost loved ones. The terrorist attack in 2001 was something that brought us all together emotionally, but the soul group consists of those who were there or immediately impacted by the tragedy.

Another term that is thrown around in the metaphysical and spiritual community is "twin flame" (also known as twin souls), which is frequently used as synonym for soul mate. But in reality, it is a different entity. Twin flames are two complete souls that were once unified, but chose to split to further the growth of each. It is believed that although twin flames often choose to incarnate and come to earth at the same time, they usually don't do so in the same geographic area. The idea is that each soul will have very specific, distinct, different experiences that they will, ultimately, bring back to each other when they ascend (often thought to happen at the same time) and arrive back on the other side.

An example of twin flames are Elizabeth Taylor and Michael Jackson. They went through a lot of similar experiences and had common bonds. Looking at the two, you wouldn't think they'd be such close friends, but they really did share a bond in life. They were child actors, had very public and difficult relationships, were constantly in the media, and had their lives examined, judged, and critiqued by all. Twin flames may not resemble each other in any way, but the connection goes much deeper and farther back.

For soul mates, who are thought to have lifetimes together, geographic and physical closeness is important. Because the Universe is so expansive and there is so much to understand and learn, we like to have one, particular individual (read: soul) to have not only as a partner in growth, but also to share the experience with. They comfort us and have an inherent understanding of who and what we are (embracing the idea that we have had multiple lives together). Although they may not currently be a soul mate, we designate them as such. So, through the history, experience, trials, and tribulations, we deem them worthy and choose each other.

I wish I could give you a telltale sign that you have made contact with your soul mate. Wouldn't it be cool if, say, all of a sudden your eyes changed color or some other physical transformation occurred? But the spiritual world doesn't work like that. It's that fantastic free will that we're all gifted with. We need to find out and determine, ourselves, if we have made that Divine connection. Regardless, it's nothing to worry about. Life goes on with or without a soul mate. What is so nifty about the spiritual world is it doesn't need credit, applause, or distinction. It's just happy that you're trying!

One final note on the aspect of soul mates not being romantic partners. In twenty years of providing readings to lovely people all over the world, I have come across a dozen or so who are romantically involved with their soul mate. However, I have had the joy of connecting with countless people who have found that their mother, best friend, or someone else was working in the role all along. And they couldn't be happier!

I recently did a reading for a young woman who told me about an ex-boyfriend. She had an immediate connection with him when they had first met, but they had just broken up after a year and a half together. She was hoping they would get back together because she truly believed in her heart that he was the One—her soul mate. I, unfortunately, did not see the soul mate connection—all I saw was two people who could only be friends and would not be successful in a long-term romantic relationship. My client was a bit heartbroken upon hearing this, but she took it on faith and we ended the reading. Two weeks later, this client emailed me and confirmed what I had told her. Since the reading she and her ex-boyfriend had started communicating again and were in the process of building a solid foundation for a lifelong non-romantic friendship, one that would support the other. Both she and the ex-boyfriend had also met other people they were interested in and were actually able to give each support and encouragement.

Although I've tried to explain to you, dear reader, what soul mates, soul groups, and twin flames are, it doesn't mean that you won't find a different definition out there. And that's okay. You have to determine for yourself what these things are, and even if you believe in the existence. Really, it's simply something to contemplate. Ultimately, your soul knows what it needs to do and where it needs to go. Having the soul mate with you can help in learning the lessons here, but it's not the last piece of the puzzle.

Three

Settling Versus the One

What the heck is the One? When folks use the term "the One," I believe it to mean that one person that we will spend the rest of our lives with. What people fail to understand is that a lifelong partner doesn't mean everlasting, unending bliss. We'd probably all agree that there isn't a perfect relationship. Heck. We're not perfect ourselves, so how could we expect two people in a dynamic relationship to get it right all the time. I think it's unfortunate many people believe that lifelong equals the One. I know far too many good people in very long-term, and quite unhappy, relationships. This is something to keep in mind because no matter how much you think the person is the One, first and foremost you need to consider your own happiness.

I think it's important to pick generally and choose wisely. You can quote me on that. What I mean is that you should, absolutely, know those things that you must have in a relationship. And whatever those things are, that's your decision. No one can tell you what is important to you. However, don't make your list so long that it excludes 90 percent of the population. Maybe have three to five things that are non-negotiable. From there, be open to whatever comes your way. Use those few things to pick but choose that relationship with wisdom and flexibility. If it's not on the short list of deal breakers (we talk about those in chapter 4), be open to potential. Give them a chance. And, more importantly, give yourself a chance to be the One to another person.

Some realistic ideals that people can focus on and help create the perfect combination for the One include living in the same geographical area, belonging to the same religion, and sharing a similar work ethic. Some unrealistic ideals that people can get caught up in but really don't matter include money, looks, occupation, and social status. If you are a small-town girl, there's a very small chance that a multimillionaire in a Porsche is going to sweep you off your feet.

And that leads me to my next point…

What are you doing to be the One for someone else? Let's face it. Not one of us could probably win first place in a Best in a Relationship contest. We all have our silly quirks and nuances. But because we know ourselves and live in our own skin, we give ourselves a pass. There's nothing wrong with that. It's human nature. However, being so critical of potential mates, we must put up the mirror and examine our own lives objectively. If you're looking for that perfect physical specimen, you need to make sure you, yourself, are getting on the treadmill consistently. Do you want someone to take care of you? What would you do to nurture that other soul? Relationships aren't all about what is coming your way. It's about the give and take. What you are looking for needs to be found within.

Which leads me to this: No one, and I mean no one, will fix you. Getting into a relationship in a troubled state doesn't make things all better. If you are dealing with uncommonly difficult monetary issues, kid problems, or family problems, before you dive into the dating pool, you must first—at the least—have identified the issues and started implementing a solution. Don't buy into the mindset that everything would be hunky-dory if only you had a significant other.

It won't. In fact, bringing another impartial individual into the equation may actually exacerbate the issue. Think of it this way: Any problem you are experiencing is completely understood by you and only you. Another individual may come in and be pretty critical of that situation and, ultimately, of you and your actions. So get your stuff straight. The upcoming relationship will be better off for it.

Now, conceding isn't giving up. We're not perfect. We all have our flaws. Understanding and respecting others' habits isn't a bad thing. In fact, in any relationship, no matter how wonderful, we need to pick our battles. Give and take is the name of the game whether the relationship is just beginning or you have been married for forty-five years. Honoring our partner's ways and means is really a sign of respect and growth within us. And when we do that for others, then our own quirks can be loved and embraced.

People may associate settling with sacrificing. Settling really means growth and moving on. Wars are settled. Court cases are settled. There isn't anything wrong with settling. In fact, what we settle for may be the best thing for us. It's as simple as this: Although we may want the delicious bacon cheeseburger all the time, we all know that there are better, more nutritious options. (I can relate anything to food.) Nature created them for balance. Sometimes the bacon cheeseburger is okay—and needed. However, we should not live on them (even if we want to). The same thing goes with settling. As we get older, what we would have considered settling in our younger years, becomes exactly the most perfect solution. So, as you continue on your dating path, continually re-evaluate what works for you and what doesn't. You may find that over time, things shift.

Let me share a story...Shortly after I was married, I was out with a single girlfriend. We were at a bar having drinks and a darling guy approached my pal and started talking to her. She quickly shut him down and turned her back on him. I was astonished. He seemed cute, funny, and genuinely interested. When I asked her why the abrupt dismissal, she told me one thing: "I didn't like his shoes."

Was my friend right in doing what she did? She didn't string this guy along. She quickly ended the interaction. This guy knew, within ten minutes, that he wasn't going to be getting a phone number, wasn't going home with her—heck, he wasn't even going to get to dance with her and buy her a cocktail afterward. She ruled this guy out by one simple, shallow-as-it-may-be, issue. Could he have been the One? Not in her eyes. In her eyes, shoes equal much more than just fashion sense. Did I think she was crazy? Heck yeah. But her rules for dating are hers alone. When she eventually did meet the man she married, she didn't care about his shoes. He wore sneakers all the time. What she worried about with one guy didn't matter with the one she fell for.

Maybe it's just a matter of growing up. It's great to live in a fantasy world where that prince or princess rides up out of nowhere and sweeps us off our feet. But it's not very likely. Get over the idea that they might just show up on your doorstep, too. You've got to work for it, people. Although the gift of love is certainly divine, the Universe will provide equal to the work that we put in, same as our career. I hate to make relationships sound like work, but they are. And yes, our potential partners should love us for who we are, but we need to make the external reflect the beauty on the inside. So don't think you can go around looking like a schlub and expect a Brad Pitt-esque dude or Angelina Jolie–type of chick to see the inner you!

The moral of this story is to really decipher what you need versus what you want. What is most important and relevant in a long-term, happy relationship? Six-pack abs or someone who is loving and faithful? We all would probably have the same answer. Try this exercise: Write down your ideals and then think of how much that will matter fifty years down the road. Looks, titles, and many other things fade with time. What you will be left with is character, integrity, loyalty, and, hopefully, love. And that, my lovely readers, is what it's all about.

Four

Deal Breakers

Deal breakers are those little things that we can't live without. Or need to live without, depending on the issue. We all have 'em. For some, they might be a seemingly small issue that has big significance, like needing popcorn to watch a movie. For others, it may be as major as religion. Either way, we all have those few things, regardless of love for another, that we need for ourselves first and foremost. What you need to figure out is what they really, truly, deeply are.

Honesty

Most of us could agree that honesty is of paramount importance, but along with honesty, comes its first cousin: trust. Without honestly, there is no basis for a long-lasting, loving relationship. It just can't be. Just like we can't live without food, a good relationship cannot survive without honesty, and ultimately, trust. If you find out that there are little lies in the beginning, you can count on bigger, bolder lies as the relationship progresses. It really is an equation. Unfortunately (and we've all been there), one lie often has to be covered with another equal or larger lie. And so it snowballs. So, guys and gals, if you're busting your new romantic partner on an untruth, however small it may be, think twice about proceeding forward. If you do, chances are you will come to regret it.

Cheating

Since we're talking about trust, let's touch on the issue of cheating. Believe it or not, cheating isn't a deal breaker for everyone. Some may find it within their heart to not undo a relationship because their partner stepped outside of it. Personally, and I'm only speaking for me, it is absolutely something that I could not live with. I don't believe I have that kind of forgiveness or compassion in my heart. However, where you stand on that issue is something you'll have to determine on your own. For some, under certain conditions, it can be explained and forgiven. For others, it's an absolute. My advice, and I could not suggest it enough, is to look within and determine where you are at with that issue at the beginning of every new romantic relationship. When you find the answer within yourself, have that conversation with your new interest. You may find that you're on the same page. You may find that you have very different perspectives. Whatever the case, you should have the discussion. If you find that you don't agree, let the relationship go.

Sexuality

I'm just putting this out there. You need to do the same. In this day and age of people being polyamorous, bisexual, transgendered, etc., you need to be upfront with what you are okay with, what you're about, and what you're into. Okay. This may not be first-date talk. But I definitely think it's fodder for a second date. Beyond that, you are just hiding yourself. Surprisingly, we are becoming a pretty worldly society thanks to global news and the Internet. We understand the dimensions to love and where it takes people. So, whether you are a mainstream, one-on-one, heterosexual sort of person or someone who is open to other concepts of love, be committed to the decision. And have the courage and freedom to convey it.

Politics

Another hot topic is politics. Yep. That stuff that we see on CNN and FOX News day in and day out. Believe it or not, behind money (the number one strain on relationships), studies have shown that differences in political views can cause great hardship in marriages. Now, more often than not, our political views are developed and determined a little later in life—oftentimes after marriage. However, if you developed your political viewpoint early, during your dating years—put it out there! Although many of us were taught never to speak about sex, religion, or politics, if it's one of your core convictions, it needs to be communicated. Now, communication doesn't mean debating, preaching, or convincing. Communication is just telling a potential suitor your perspective. That's all.

And since I just mentioned religion ...

Religion

Your belief system is just that—yours. Whether or not you subscribe to one of the world's major religions or find that simple spirituality is more your cup of tea, you need to let that be known. Can a Fundamentalist Baptist and a Unitarian get along? Most certainly. Can they have a romantic relationship in which they fulfill and nurture each other without stepping on personal belief systems? That depends on each individual. The biggest hurdle is determining what is going to happen long term. When and if children come into the mix, how will they be raised? Are they baptized in one faith or the other? Who wins? While relationships are unquestionably based on compromise, this is one of those issues that is so deeply individual, we rarely want to concede on any level. That's why knowing where you stand and determining how much you are willing to compromise is essential before entering into anything long term.

Children

Another major deal breaker is children—to have them or not. Now, sometimes this is out of our hands no matter how much we would like to be parents. Unfortunately, biology has a hand in this. However, for most, it's determined by the couple. Are you willing to be a parent? I know, for some, as crazy as this may sound, it's determined by who we end up partnering with. I've known several women who, when single, never thought of themselves as mothers and were quite adamant about not having kids. However, when they found themselves in that loving, long-term commitment, their thoughts changed. Fortunately for us, all of the deal breakers can be changed, altered, or added as we ourselves change. Children are a prime example. A dear client of mine married a man who had children from a previous relationship and had no desire to have any more. My client, at that time, was perfectly fine with not having children, and they married and had a fabulous start to their life together. But as time went on, she realized that she really did want to have children. When she mentioned this to her husband, he said, "We already discussed this. I've already raised two children. I'm done with that part of my life."

When I tuned in to this relationship all I could see was brokenheartedness over not being able to deepen the bond with her husband by having a child with him. She loved her stepchildren deeply, but desired to bear one of her own, something she and her husband would create together out of their love for one another. However, she knew going in that her husband did not share that same desire. Although her wants and needs changed since the beginning of the relationship, her husband's desires had not, and this put a great deal of strain on the marriage. It got so bad that my client turned to prescription drugs to fill the void. This in turn required a great deal of counseling and therapy. In the end, my client decided her husband and her marriage were more important than anything else and she came out the other end clean, happy, and closer to her husband than ever before. Now she laughs about this period in her life and jokes about how buying and raising a couple of dogs was the best therapy she ever gave herself.

Geography

It's happened to many of us. We meet a stranger, get all those butterflies and feel a sense of attraction only to find that the individual lives five hundred miles away. Geography can be a deal breaker. Let's be real. Love is love beyond culture, background, and class. However, it makes life a lot easier if they are at least semi-local. This isn't to say that you don't have the bandwidth to handle something more geographically impaired. You very well may. As with all of the above deal breakers, it's something you may want to consider prior to investing emotions with a new love. Are you okay with the two-hour drive to see one another? Or, maybe, worse yet, it's a situation where you can only see each other once a month? Can that be the foundation for a solid, committed relationship? That's up to you.

Moral Objections

What if your new love works in a field that you feel compromises your morality or integrity? Think about it. As we all know and I've stated many times before, we live in an ever-expanding world. Along with that expansion comes various careers that wouldn't be considered mainstream. Heck, look at what I do for a living. Being a psychic is not exactly understood in the same manner as a dentist or accountant. What if you find yourself caring for someone who runs an adult website? Or maybe the person you're falling for works for a tobacco company. What are you okay with? Ultimately, it's the person who should be evaluated and not their occupation. However, sometimes it's hard to discern between the two.

Finances

Of course, if we're thinking about the job, we have to talk about financial situations. I don't believe that money can buy you happiness. But it does bring freedom and ultimately, that freedom can make things a lot easier. Getting involved with someone with a sketchy financial history can make life really messy, especially if you happen to marry that someone. Most of us have had hiccups at some point with our finances. That's not what I'm talking about. I'm talking about major debt, foreclosures, bankruptcies, that sort of thing. As I write this, the economy is not in the best shape, so we have a great deal of understanding as to the why's and how's of subpar financial situations.

However, we can make the choice not to combine our financial situations with someone who has been or is currently in a monetary pickle. This isn't a topic that needs to be discussed on a first date. In fact, I would say hold off on this conversation for a bit. Wait until the fifth or the sixth date. Money, right next to health, is an extremely personal topic and one that isn't necessary to divulge right up front. But it is something to think about before investing emotionally.

Hygiene and Health

This could be a gross one . . . hygiene and health. No one likes to be with someone who is smelly. It's really just that simple. Take care of yourself. Brush your teeth. Clean under your fingernails. All that good stuff that mom taught you as a toddler. Of course, if you don't have hygiene working for you, you probably won't have to worry about the relationship. No one will want to hang out long enough to become invested. Sorry. It's a harsh world, and I'm just preaching the truth. To take this one step further, if you become engrossed in a long-term relationship, don't slack off in this area. Just because we have found love doesn't mean we can let ourselves go. Investing the time to doll up, as I like to call it, shows the other person that you still care about them.

Now, health, on the other hand, isn't so upfront. We can have scads of health issues that aren't apparent by simply looking at someone. STDs (sexually transmitted diseases) are a perfect example. I don't believe that chronic conditions should be left to be discovered months into the relationship. That could result in quite a shock to someone after they've become very emotionally attached. They weren't deceived exactly, but the full and open truth hadn't been exposed. Thankfully we live in a time where diseases of the past are easily managed and better understood. Think about what you, as a single person, are willing to live with. Be true to yourself in this arena because if you aren't, you could end up really hurting someone dear.

Habits

We all have habits. Some are good, such as being consistent about wearing your safety belt in a car or visiting the dentist every six months. Some may be not so great, like smoking cigarettes, chewing tobacco, or drinking alcohol. You may encounter, as you search for your long-term companion, an individual that indulges in an activity you don't agree with. Whether it's something that just grosses you out or is an issue of morality, take time to ponder those behaviors and determine what you can live with. Keep in mind, however, that you, and your good influence, may be just the thing to change that nasty habit! Just don't waste too much time and effort being the catalyst for that change.

Family

Believe it or not, family can and may be a deal breaker. There's a reason so for all those mother-in-law jokes. But all kidding aside, having family issues can take a toll on a relationship. Do you have a parent that is just a little too involved in your life? A major part of any relationship is the transition from immediate family (parents and siblings) being your only family to allowing your partner to create and be that new family, adding in new traditions, belief systems, and protocol. Another potential issue is the behavior of family members. As much as career, financial issues, and religion are part of your immediate relationship, they become an adjacent issue when involving the family. An extended family's opinions and beliefs can become a major source of conflict. Our families are an extension of ourselves. As the relationship becomes deeper, we need to connect the new part of us (that other individual we are committed to) to our history and background (our family). And therein can lie issues, which are just one more thing to add to the list of items to work through prior to allowing yourself to grow deeper in any relationship.

Abuse

One thing that we can all agree on as a deal breaker is any form of abuse. Don't tolerate it for one moment. No one deserves physical, mental, or emotional abuse under any circumstance. If you find yourself in an abusive situation, the only thing to do is to get out as fast as possible. Get out for yourself and get out for the individual creating the situation. It's only then that the healing can begin. No one benefits from being tolerant of mistreatment in any form.

As you can see, many deal breakers are tolerable depending on the person involved. There are variables in every situation.

For example, when I was younger, I absolutely hated guys who chewed tobacco. The vision of them spitting into an old soda bottle is just disgusting. But when I met Bobby, guess what he did? He chewed tobacco. It's disgusting, but in the grand scheme of things, it was something I could tolerate. I wasn't pleased, and I double- and triple-checked my soda bottle every time I took a drink because I was deathly afraid of ingesting disgusting chaw spit, but he was too awesome to kick to the curb for something so trivial. Thankfully that addiction has passed, for the most part. It's something that I vowed never to tolerate, but I did for the right fella.

It's handy to think about what you would do, ahead of time, in any given situation, and how much you could tolerate something you disliked. Be prepared. By doing this, we set standards for ourselves and our relationships before becoming overly committed. A great exercise is to write out a list of small, medium, and large deal breakers. It allows you to include the petty things that would be annoying but not horrible, like nose hair, and highlight the things that are more substantial, such as children, religion, geography, and all the rest of the big ones.

Five

The Dork Within

So much of the relationship process starts with dating. Even if you're one of those people who dives head first into relationships, it all still starts with a first date. Whether it is dinner, visiting a museum, coffee, or a movie, the process needs to start somewhere, so here we go...

I'm a big advocate of being exactly who you are right from the get-go. Our flaws and foibles make us who we are. This is how we are different and unique. Of course, at first we're all on our best behavior. That's just human nature. Sure, we do try to impress and chew with our mouths closed. However, beyond the pleasantries, we just need to throw caution to the wind and simply be ourselves. Seems like a pretty simple idea, doesn't it?

It's not. For a lot of folks, we make ourselves, or, maybe better said, portray ourselves as something we are not. Ladies and gentlemen, this is a bad idea. Oh, such a very, super, bad idea.

If you pretend to be something you are not, like a whitewashed wall, who you really are will eventually come through and may surprise the person you're trying to impress. Here's a little theory that I've cooked up over the last several years speaking to both men and women about who they date and end up in relationships with (get that pen and paper ready, because it may rock your world):

We all like a little crazy.

That's it. No one wants (as I like to call it) a Ward and June Cleaver relationship forever. They're boring. They may be incredibly healthy. They may be comfortable. And they're definitely stable. I'm sure they'll have a few laughs now and again. But, overall, it's boring. We get enough boring at work; we get some boring from family too. We even find boring within our friendships. We don't need it in our relationships that hopefully become our home life.

Now, when I use the term crazy, I obviously don't mean it literally. Don't date serial killers, child molesters, or pyromaniacs. What I'm saying is that we all have quirks. Most of us have something we obsess over a bit. Phobias happen. We may even have things in our past that we're not proud of and have had to make some sort of public restitution for. That's okay. That's character, and frankly, it makes for interesting conversation when courting.

I want to talk about the sorts of things that I really feel need to be disclosed. Most of these aren't deal breakers, but may cause friction or an awkward moment or two when getting to know one another. Let's dive in.

Sports freaks, yes, I'm looking at you Mr. or Ms. Five or Six Fantasy Leagues. It's great that you have a hobby and even better that it's aboveboard and law abiding. However, if it takes up several hours a week all year long, it really needs to be discussed. If you paint any part of your body to go to the game, you should talk about it. You haven't washed the team's jersey/T-shirt/sweats in three years because you're superstitious about them getting to the playoffs? Bring it up. You're a fan. We can all understand that. But if you're going to pick your wedding date to coordinate with your favorite player's birthday, you may want to get your partner to buy in. That's a little bit crazy, but something that we can all cope with—but only if we understand and know all about it up front, in advance.

We all know ourselves, and we know how we act and react to all sorts of situations. We know under pressure and strain how we handle it and where we turn. So do not kid yourself. And especially don't play around with others' thoughts and feelings. Although dating and being in any relationship is about discovering the other's foibles, if you know you have a temper, it's going to do an extreme amount of good if you let the interested party know that. If you know that you're passive-aggressive and maybe not the fairest arguer out there, well that is just good information to pass along. Do you shut down and hole up when confronted? There's nothing wrong with that, but before a situation arises, why not share that tidbit of information? By doing this, you're letting the other person know that you A: care enough to share a vulnerability, and B: are potentially squelching an issue that could further the argument or incident. We all have our quirks. When you share yours, it becomes the kind of crazy we can or should all embrace.

A crazy that 98 percent of us can relate to (no pun intended—you'll see what's coming) is the crazy family kind of crazy. If we don't have immediate-family drama, we have extended-family drama. If you don't have either, you must be an alien. I joke. All of us, even if we're the small fraction of a percent that doesn't have family issues, can sympathize. We see it all around us whether on the news or hearing it from friends. If you have your own family drama, you may want to disclose it pretty early on. It's unfortunate that familial issues can affect us so deeply on an emotional level. But they do. Someone can do something out of pure humor or innocence and have it turn out, due to unforeseen family issues, very sour. Using a specific word that was negatively used in your household can trigger a response that an outsider wouldn't see coming. Or maybe it's trust. Due to the high level of divorce in the United States, many children of divorce have abandonment issues as adults. Fortunately for us, as I mentioned prior, most all of us can relate. So what you think may be your family's crazy just may be another's normal everyday understanding.

The bottom line here is to not only share your own personal version of crazy, but to think about, specifically, the kind of crazy you are okay with. It's these varying degrees of experience, quirkiness, and idiosyncrasies that make up the population today. And embrace the fact that nobody loves boring! It doesn't matter what kind of a freak you are, somebody will love your freak.

Six

....

They Don't Care What You Wear or What You Drive

It's unbelievable how much thought we put into how we present ourselves when we're out in the dating world. Hair, makeup (that applies mainly to gals, but with the new trend of guyliner, I'm keeping it gender neutral), clothes—not to mention the time that we put into thinking about conversations, opening lines, and what we're willing to divulge about our lives. So let's cut through the BS. Let's get to the heart of what really matters and what couldn't matter less. Those are the lovely myths and misnomers of the dating world.

The Ride

I'm sure that there are girls out there who really do care what vehicle a boy is driving. But what we might find interesting or enchanting for a moment does not a relationship make. Car schmar. Although most of us, regardless of gender, can appreciate a fancy car, never in my thirty-plus years have I known any gal to date a guy just on that alone. Having a car in order to get around is pretty important. Type, model, or make is pretty trivial. And let's face it, if she really just cares about the car, is that the kind of girl you really want to invest your time, money, and gas on?

The Clothes

Conversely, ladies, guys really don't care what you're wearing. Outside of being clean and somewhat put together, they aren't noticing whether the frock is Prada or JC Penney. It's all about how you carry yourself. The time-tested, classic, standard will always be proven—guys like girls in a plain old T-shirt and jeans rather than a cocktail dress. Can they appreciate the time and effort into getting dressed up and putting on something more revealing? Sure. But when it comes down to it, a white shirt and blue jeans will win every time. While we are talking about external appearances, I can say that not one time in my extremely informal poll (via social media and various nights out with friends), did I hear "I really like a girl that wears a lot of make-up." In fact, it was quite the opposite. With cosmetics, less is more. Now, that doesn't mean that less is none. Less is a look of a clean face with enhancement (as I like to call it).

Name-dropping

We like to associate ourselves with other people. It helps communicate our rank, class, and status in life. Not to mention that it can create a bond between two people if they have a common acquaintance. However, that's where the coolness ends. Don't date someone for who they know. Mentioning celebrities, sport figures, and stars doesn't cost anything and is pretty unverifiable. Who knows, in this day and age of Twitter and Facebook, a celeb may have given a shout-out, but that sure doesn't mean they're friends—or even acquaintances. Unfortunately we live in a time where we are impressed by notoriety and somehow admire those in the media. Don't get swept up with these brushes with fame. In romantic relationships, it's who you are, not who you know.

Big, um, Hands

You were probably expecting something other than hands. Guys, I hate to break it to you, but we're not going to date you or reject you due to size…of hands. (If you're not getting the innuendo here, just move on to the next paragraph.) Don't try, in any way, to express your physical prowess. It's just gross. Not to mention awkward, off-putting, and creepy. We don't need to know your shoe size either. Locker room–type talk needs to stay in the locker room.

Your Past

The saying goes, once a cheat, always a cheat. Although I'm not fond of cheating, this little cliché isn't always the case. Unfortunately, with cheating, most often it's more about the entire situation/relationship rather than the individual. Just ask any cheater. They'll be the first to tell you that the relationship had problems far beyond (and likely far before) the cheating. Let's face it, if we live by this rule, we'd all have scarlet letters on our sweaters. Who hasn't had a cheating moment in high school? Or maybe even college. But you can't take that with you into your adult life. We all know those people that are serial cheaters. That's not who we're talking about here. Remember to judge every person and every potential relationship as if it's your first.

Job Titles and Prestige

Don't try to impress with a job title, bogus or otherwise. I know gals who are deeply in love with worm farmers (Yes. There's such a thing.) And I know guys who are completely entranced by the gal at the dry cleaner. Conversely, there are women who can't stand their doctor husband and guys that can barely live with their attorney wife. Careers and titles don't necessarily define people. And they certainly don't define character or integrity. Who doesn't know someone with a lofty professional label, but is, ultimately, a total ass?

What Do We Care About?

So, if we aren't supposed to care about looks, money, cars, clothes, or connections, what's left? I'm glad you asked.

Everything else is just a thing. It's not you. What is important is that you are exactly who you are. Nothing of what makes you who you are can be purchased in a store: your soul, sense of humor, personality. Be up front and honest with people, and who cares what clothes you're wearing or what car you're driving; those are just material things that do not matter, nor do they make someone perfect. No one is perfect. We are who we are, so just be you. We are beings of life, not of things.

Guys: The number one thing that has been proven, over and over in poll after poll is that women love a sense of humor, period. Ask any gal on the street and you can rest assured that's what you'll hear. We love guys that will make us laugh. You don't have to be a stand-up comedian. That's what's so great about it. Humor is relative and as such, individual in every person. So, there's someone out there for every type of laugh. Dry humor, there's a gal for that. Naughty or vulgar jokes, some girl out there loves it. Keep that in mind. Open with a witty comment or joke and you'll have our attention. You don't have to be the class clown or Chris Rock. You will find someone who loves your sense of humor and wackiness.

Gals: The number one thing that guys want is honesty, which goes right along with trustworthiness. Believe it or not, when a guy gets cheated on, they take it harder than women. I've seen it time and time again in my practice. Although a woman becomes wounded initially, we seem to move through that and heal more rapidly. Guys, on the other hand, initially seem to be tough and a little callous. Then the hurt sets in days or weeks later, only to linger for quite a while. So don't mislead those boys. Don't laugh at their jokes if you don't think they are funny. Don't lead them on because you don't have anything better to do. If it's not working for you, let it go. (We talk more about that in another section of the book.)

The main thing that I hear from both genders is that we all want consistency. Here's why: Inconsistency makes us feel as if we're going crazy. It makes us feel like we didn't remember something correctly or behaved poorly in the past. We love a habit. We like to know what to expect. That way, we can behave in a way that has had a proven response. So it's pretty easy. In the same way that one plus one always equals two, we'd like the ebb and flow of our relationships to be somewhat of a pattern.

Seven

The Most Important Attributes

There are a lot of things that attract us to the opposite sex. And make no mistake; we all have a type. Of course, there are different combinations and versions of that type, but we sure have 'em. That all being said, there are a few things we all look for and find attractive in a potential partner or spouse. And believe it or not, looks and/or appearance are not even in the top three.

I don't think any gal really believes that it's all about the make-up, hair, or clothes when attracting a suitor. However, it seems to really be where we put our focus. We girls think we must have just the right shoes and our hair coiffed just so. Spray tan applied in just the right shade. I think we all know the truth. Boys couldn't give a rip. Now, they don't want us to be smelly, haggard, or outwardly offensive. But simply being presentable works. Do they notice when we go all out and doll up? Sure. Do they expect that 100 percent of the time? Nope. When I took a random poll, once again using my social media network, the girl-next-door look won out over glamour girl, goth girl, athletic girl, and hippie chick—in a landslide. Boys (my generic term for males regardless of age) love the gal in a T-shirt and jeans. They're not looking for labels, trends, or fashion moments. Boys like unfussy. It's about being the all-American girl ready to take a hike, go to a club, or see a concert.

Which leads me to my next point: Boys want the Mary Ann, not the Ginger. For those of you not familiar, I'm referencing *Gilligan's Island*, a TV show that aired from 1964 to 1967. It portrayed some archetypical characters stranded on an island. Although the reference is a major stereotype, it still fits and applies today. Mary Ann was the farmer's daughter, the girl-next-door type. She was approachable, cute, and down-to-earth. Ginger on the other hand was the va-va-voom starlet. She had perfect hair, the come-hither voice and sparkly dresses. (Although it was only a three-hour tour, somehow she had packed a full wardrobe.) But here is the secret: Boys interpret glammed-up girls as labor intensive. And let's face it; although the boy himself may be quite high maintenance, they all want girls who are not afraid to get dirty. (Don't go to the naughty version. This is the literal meaning of dirty.)

Although boys have an understanding that most of us want to play dress-up now and again, they don't really care for that scenario. Think of how much they crab when they simply have to wear a tie. The same thought process transcends to women. If it's more work to put on a tie, it's going to be more work, more time, and more trouble for a girl to get her face on. They'd rather just take it easy and make things as simple as possible.

Now for the boys ...

I know it's hard for girls to believe, but with the onset of the metrosexual, it's getting easier to comprehend—boys care about how they look. But boys need to understand that, we, as women, also don't really care. More than anything, attraction is about how you make us feel. If you men haven't gotten the memo, women are about the emotion. That's why we talk about our feelings so darn much. Duh! Although we like pretty, shiny things, it really comes down to how we react to what you say and do.

Not only don't we care about how you look, we really do not care about what kind of car you drive either. And beyond giving you a stable income and ability to live on your own, we really don't care about your profession. Of course, we like to know and see that you have plans, dreams, and goals for the future, not your fancy job title. Prestige and awe is temporary. What makes a successful relationship are the thoughts, feelings, and caring between the two individuals. So the moral of the story is to stop BS-ing women when trying to meet them. Do you really want us to be attracted to you (temporarily) by a false pretense that really doesn't matter anyway? And, frankly, it's pretty douchey to open any conversation by bragging about your job, whether it's dentist, doctor, or door maker.

Again, it's about how guys make us feel. Specifically, if you really want the inside track, just make us laugh. I've said this before, but it's worth repeating: Humor is major. Once again, I asked the ladies in my trusted social media network what they look for most in a man. Absolute numero uno answer was humor. It seems being funny trumps good looking and wealthy every time. Not that those things aren't important because they are. If a boy can make us laugh, our heart belongs to him and all other things just fall to the wayside. Humor is endearing. We all know that there are going to be rough sides to relationships no matter how perfect we think we are. So, on a deep soul level, we know if you can make us laugh, we'll get through those troubled times with you standing by our side.

One more thing for the stronger (physically speaking) of the species: we gals are looking for understanding. (They may take away my girl card for sharing such a substantial secret with the men folk.) You men thinking that we need apologies. We don't, unless you mean them, and they are necessary. BUT more than anything, and I can't stress this enough, women want to be understood. Say those words to us and everything else can be reconciled and figured out. If you understand why we are upset (this includes angry, frustrated, in a general bad mood) we'll heal and move through the issue exponentially faster. I promise.

I cannot tell you how many times, in reading after reading, women have confessed to me that if their partner would just get them, they could move on and create a happier, more fulfilling relationship. Boys, don't think for one minute that the relationship isn't guided by the girl. It is. Deal with it. Understanding someone goes so much further than just the isolated apology. It speaks to the connection between the two individuals and gives accountability if the situation arises again. An apology is simply that. An "I'm sorry." Understanding says that we have processed the issue and realize what will happen if the same actions are taken again. When you do that, it signals that you get us and understand why we reacted the way we did. That's what's important to us.

A final note for both men and women: It's often said that we don't want to marry our parents. That's because we often vividly remember their bad characteristics. On the other hand, we, as people are naturally attracted to something familiar—good or bad. To me, this simply means we want to do better for ourselves and potentially for our children by avoiding our parents' flaws and foibles. So it's true in the sense that we should take note of those traits of our parents that we're not so fond. But we should also identify the good stuff. Then when you are seeking a partner keep those traits in mind. And remember, just because something is familiar (emotional distance, bad habits, etc.), doesn't mean it's good.

Eight

Bad Boys and Girls

Those bad boys and those bad girls; we all know one when we see them. Who hasn't had the Betty vs. Veronica debate? They're portrayed in television and in the movies, often corrupting the innocent one that they set their sights on, and we love it. We love the idea of drama, and the potential for change . . . in either direction. We adore that little devil who turns into a little angel. We love it even more when we see someone let loose and tap into their wild side. But is that wild child for you?

We are drawn to those that may be less than beneficial for us for countless reasons. It could be as simple as the excitement. Walking on the edge, knowing we could fall at any moment is pretty darn exciting—especially if we've lived our lives as upstanding, follow-the-rules type of folks.

Maybe we want to heal the badness out of someone. We, sometimes, associate bad coming from a previous, harsh experience or existence. So, we want a fixer-upper. We see the potential and greatness within them. We want to take away the pain and the hurt of what has come before. Or maybe, just maybe we recognize something within ourselves. Although we couldn't bring ourselves to just let it loose, that other person may provide just the excuse.

When I was in high school, I was an angel. I never had detention, I didn't skip school, I didn't do drugs, and I never broke curfew. I was the typical Midwestern good girl. But then I met a bad boy. He was the poster child for who you don't want your daughter to date. (My poor mother!) You name it, he (a high school dropout) did it: drugs, alcohol, questionable escapades. Why was I attracted to him? I don't know. There was something about him living by his own means. He didn't have a lot of support from his family, and they didn't care what trouble he got into. Compared to his siblings, he was a good kid. The relationship was intense. I had a headache for two years. I cried every day. I tried to get an intervention with his parents so they could stop him from drinking and drugging, but he didn't listen. I worried about him so much that he ended up breaking up with me. He didn't want a girlfriend who nagged about and condemned his behavior. It was awful all around. The main lesson I learned was to not date alcoholic drug users. No really, after all was said and done, I realized I had value. I realized that I needed to be treated well. I realized I loved his family more than I loved him, but the constant excitement and craziness became too much.

So maybe we, by dating the bad boy or girl, are just projecting something within ourselves. You get addicted to the crazy and are caught up in the whirlwind of their life. Crazy becomes normal. It's hard to determine what is real and what isn't. Crazy is what you are pushed to; it's not an authentic emotion. It's a reaction. And it's hard to break out of that cycle. You may want to ponder that notion. If there is something that you just need to express and this other person is giving you a venue, why not just go after it yourself? Although we live in a world that is becoming more and more connected, it's also giving us opportunities to have experiences and connect with people outside of the norm, whatever your personal normal may be. With the virtual world, we can be and do almost anything or anyone.

What defines someone as bad? Heck, that could be a book in and of itself. It could just be attitude. Nothing turns on the typical guy or gal like someone who doesn't give a crap. Not giving a crap is pretty freeing…in some instances. When they don't return phone calls, emails, and texts, then it's pretty darn annoying. The badness could be from a sense of style. As superficial as it may be, and crazy as it might seem, presenting yourself a bit out of the mainstream can be exciting. Think about gals that really…ahem…put themselves out there. I'm trying to be tactful. They don't care if their skirts are too short or their necklines are too low. It's a statement. They're going to get looks of lust and looks of scorn. And they're okay with all of it.

Believe it or not, we still live in a world where badness can be simply a faith, culture, or geographic background. Seems a little antiquated in this day and age, but it's still out there. This ideal is predominantly perpetuated by very traditional families with limited viewpoints. If your version of bad is limited by what your family thinks is bad, I recommend this: GET OVER IT. The world is getting smaller every day. We don't have the barriers to diversity anymore, so we need to embrace people from all walks of life. Don't allow a familial conviction to dictate who you are going to love.

Of course there are deeper forms of bad, like criminals and such. But let's face it. Our good sense usually tells us to stay away from the truly evil.

In some ways, bad can be good. If you are just too much of a goody-goody, a little bad may be just what the doctor ordered. For those who really live life reined in, dating someone with tattoos or a mischievous history may do you some good! Life is about the experience. Those we date and have relationships with give us that experience without having to go through the trials and tribulations ourselves. We can learn through them, from the good and the bad. Not to mention, opposites attract! Where you may be less spontaneous, your partner might bring that zest for life and joie de vivre back into your world! So it's not all wrong to dip your toes into the tempting pool of badness.

Perhaps the interest in the rebel vibe is just the challenge of getting noticed by them. Maybe you want to tame that wild side and settle them down a bit. Although most of us would agree that the chase is great fun, you have to remember that the chase doesn't make a relationship. It's a moment in time amid something longer term. And even if they're bad, they have feelings too. It's not fair to pursue anyone, bad or good, then get bored and move on after you've attracted their attention. Be certain that your intentions, if choosing to pursue the bad boy or girl, are honorable.

Part of the attraction may be the idea that we can tame the crazy, bad behavior out of 'em. If that concept seems attractive to you, let me share this thought: What happens after the wildness has left the building? Are you then left with a boring, otherwise uninteresting individual? Then what? You've not only deflated the relationship, but possibly changed someone into something they are not. Not only that, but you wasted time and effort that could have been focused on finding a more productive, realistic relationship.

Maybe those baddies are just more sensitive? It's a theory. It's not that they mean to be bad or intentionally project a bad vibe. It's their circumstance, past, and/or history. They may be wounded from what they've experienced. That, at least in part, is probably true. Sexy as the wound may be, you have to understand the proverbial baggage that goes along with that. There might be familial issues, maybe financial issues to boot. Not to mention the hurt may stem from a past romantic relationship that your potential partner may just not be over. So, vulnerable as they may be in their badness, think about how much you may, or may not, want to take on.

But hey, what about the good guy or good gal? Far too often we overlook those that are sweet, stable, and emotionally available, and . . . SHOCKER . . . interested in us as well! We don't find them exciting enough. If they want us, why would we want them? Too nice equals boring—we all know it, so I will just say it outright.

Sometimes the too-nice person who isn't your type is exactly who you should be with. A client of mine had dated a string of bad girls. Partied all night, got arrested—all-around bad behavior. A friend of his said he had the perfect girl for him. She was a financially stable homeowner with an 8 to 5 job, and she had no prior record and no children. She even had a fabulous relationship with her family. My client did not want to waste his time with a goody-goody. His previous relationship was with a part-time belly dancing moocher. But being that his buddy let him crash on his couch after the moocher kicked him out and found another fella, he figured what the hell. The blind date was a success. They instantly clicked, and he found someone who was grounded and appreciated him. She brought out his true nature, and he was finally content and happy. After struggling with happiness and contentment for so many years, he finally was able to be himself, love someone, and be loved back without excuses. And this was all from a woman who he said was not his type.

Kind reader, don't give up on the nice. Dig deep. You're going to find a little bit of bad boy or bad girl in everyone. Don't brush off or ignore a potential suitor because they can take care of themselves. Established individuals have proven themselves. They aren't the lump of coal. They're the actual diamond! Take the opportunity to learn of their success and make that an exciting part of your relationship!

Nine

Change

Within thirty seconds of mentioning my idea for this book to the public, the overwhelming request was to speak to the idea of changing someone, or more specifically, to not set out to change anyone. So, if you want to cut this section of the book short, leave with this: Don't try to change anyone into who you think they should be. It doesn't work. Pushing someone to change only creates discontent and resentment. It will never work out well. Now, if that wasn't enough for you, let's continue.

We all see the strengths and weaknesses in our chosen partners. My husband continues to leave socks lying around the house. I forget to clean the litter box. It's a give and take. All relationships have their little quirks that cause us to bicker and bitch. These aren't the type of changes I'm looking to discuss. I'm talking about the major stuff—core behaviors. Some issues may be things, that in society, we may grimace on or completely avoid. Others may be completely aboveboard activities, but are still disagreeable.

Let's take sports, for instance, to start out. Most of America is into some sort of sports team. Whether it's professional, collegiate, or a team that they, themselves, play on, it permeates society. There's nothing inherently wrong with that. It's totally legal, and it's good, clean fun. However, if someone is a fanatic, there could be a problem. One person's fanatic is another person's enthusiastic supporter. The team/sport is something that this person loves and has intertwined into their life. Is it fair to ask them to be a lesser fan? To take away a part of their life that gives them great pleasure? I don't think so. Is it fair to set up a mutual, agreed upon expectation? I say it is.

You have to always, always remember what you fell in like with. What you fell in love with tends to be more memorable, but what you fell in like with is just as important. Likes are the general, silly things about an individual that are the foundation for love. So, using that example of an extreme sports fan, that loyalty and exuberance around fun is something you totally fell in like with. If you remove that sports fan from the individual, the loyalty and exuberance will diminish or disappear entirely from the person you're looking to change.

Ultimately, if you change a like, you may very well end up changing your love. There's no getting around it. One time when I was crabbing about a relationship, a girlfriend told me, "You bought the puzzle with all the pieces." What she meant was this: You fell in love with the package. It's all wrapped up in that person. Take away one piece and the puzzle is ruined. The like is a crucial piece of the love puzzle.

But silly us. We think that if we try to change someone we're going to make them better. Have you thought that to yourself? I'm going to be insulting so get ready...How dare you. How dare you think that it's up to you to force your will on another individual? Heck, that is why our forefathers left England. It's no different than what we did to the Native American people here when we decided to settle. No one has the right to decide for another what is going to be for their own betterment. It's up to every individual to figure out, on their own time and in their own way, when and how they want to be better. Making a suggestion is one thing, but taking an active role to get them to change is pretty darn selfish when you get right down to it.

I will add a very close and personal story of my own as it relates to my marriage, the differences, and the expectations that my husband and I have. My efforts (or struggles) are ongoing and daily as I try not to change who my husband is, and the same can be said by him. I would describe myself as ambitious and have a healthy work effort in all things I do. My husband, on the other hand, has a work effort I simply cannot relate to. He is willing to sacrifice food, sleep, relationships, fun, and more all for the sake of the work itself. He and I went back and forth on this issue for the first several years of our marriage. I admit I tried to change him, and who he was, but this produced nothing but negative consequences. Only after I gave up trying to change him did things improve between us. The more I understood and accepted who he was (the guy I originally fell in love with), our differences began to disappear. To this day, Bobby and I have different expectations of one another, but thankfully we have grown up and learned to communicate better. We now focus on mutual interests instead of obsessing over the differences.

A leopard can change its spots, but a hippo isn't ever going to be a giraffe. Here is what I mean by that: We, without a doubt, can change who we are. But we're not going to become something completely different. I don't care who, what, or why you're changing. Fundamentally, you'll still be who you are. The bottom line is that any change is going to be instigated by that particular individual. And that's the way it should be.

Of course, we will all run into the folks who will communicate that they want to change and will change. And that's a good thing, something to be encouraged. However, unless you really want to set yourself up for disappointment, don't expect it to happen. At least don't expect it to happen on your terms or in your time frame. People change when they want to change. And, often, we know what we should and could change about ourselves. But a nifty part of being human, living in our own skin, is we excuse and ignore our faults and issues. Heck, we're the only ones that have to live with ourselves 100 percent of the time. So, if someone makes the promise of change, hoping for it is a wonderful thing, anticipating it is another. Be pleasantly surprised when, and if, the change happens.

We all have to remember that the only change that we have control over is how we react to others. It's not about changing the external. It's making a change within us. Our reaction to others' behavior, however, can change another individual's process. If we change how we react to an environment or situation we frequently encounter, it may just be what the doctor ordered.

If we change how we behave, that changes the entire issue, which, ultimately, warrants an entirely new response. Here is something to consider in romantic, professional, familial, and personal relationships as well. The avalanche of change has to start with you...the little snowball of transformation!

Take me, for example. I used to give my husband a very hard time during muskie-fishing season as Bobby would leave for hours, and sometimes days, on end. I'd remind him that muskie fishers are often divorced or perpetually single. My pestering, which I now realize was a weird way to indicate I missed him, turned his enjoyable hobby into a very un-fun and stressful event. Once I gave up my reactive behavior about his muskie fishing obsession, Bobby shortened his trips, took breaks during the day to call, and even texted me photos of a big fish he had just caught and released so I could share the thrill. That was the best. But the point is that things got better after my attitude toward the fishing changed, not his obsession with muskies that he came into the relationship with. I had eventually accepted that fact, and thank goodness I did, because that damn fish almost cost me my marriage!

And speaking to being the catalyst for major transformation, your decision to remove yourself from the situation may be exactly what is needed. Your departure may free up the individual to make different changes for themselves. Now, don't be lured back when and if those changes take place because, by bringing yourself back into the equation, you are creating the same scenario, drawing the same energy, which existed in the first place. So, be proud of the transition that occurred, both personally and by the other individual involved, but don't look back.

I once did a reading for a client who had serious jealousy issues and an overall lack of trust in her partner. I pointed out that she was overreacting to the most minor and ordinary things that occur in a typical or "normal" relationship. Tuning in to her partner, I did not see any reason for mistrust; he appeared to me as an honest and committed man who loved my client, and I was unable to detect any deception coming from him. I also saw very clearly that my client's behavior, stemming from her lack of trust, was constantly putting her partner on the defensive and that he was actually starting to think about leaving her.

I first provided my client the assurance that she had no reason to not trust her partner. I reminded her that she had come to me for a reason and that she would now have to have faith in the reading—at the very least she needed to attempt to utilize the behavior modification tools provided during her session. We took the next several minutes and meditated together, all the while holding hands. After a short period of time, I was able to show her what I was tuning in to about her partner. My client was able to see there was no reason to be concerned, and their relationship problems were rooted in her behavior alone. During our meditation, I was able to tune in to why my client was having such trust issues. I told her I was able to see two prior relationships that had damaged her trust in men—one from high school and one shortly after she had graduated from college. She was overwhelmed with relief to hear that her high school sweetheart had, in fact, not cheated on her like she had thought, but simply broke off the relationship for personal reasons. I confirmed what she already knew as fact about her post-college love affair—this man did cheat on her several times with several other women. These were the first steps in my client accepting that her behavior in her current relationship was the root cause issue of their problems, and she had no reason not to trust her partner. My next step was to ask my client if she would like to continue the session and try hypnotherapy, and she immediately agreed. As a board-certified hypnotherapist, I am able to modify behavior to change long-ingrained patterns such as phobias, weight issues, or substance abuse. With my client in a hypnotic state, I spent the next half hour or so reprogramming certain behaviors she displayed toward her current partner. I provided her with tools she would be able to access the next time she felt like lashing out or unnecessarily accusing her partner of misdeeds. We ended this session with some additional meditation and an aura reading. My client left feeling at peace with herself and with a certain confidence she had not felt in many years. She followed up with me a couple days later and told me that using those techniques and tools worked and helped her avoid confrontations with her partner. I did not hear from her again, but I did get an email from her partner about one month later. It was one of the most heartwarming validations I have ever received. To make a long story short, he thanked me for working with his girlfriend, stated that she was a changed person, so much so he asked her to marry him just the night before, and that she had said "YES." It's now been six years, and I still remain in contact with this couple. They remain happily married and have a four-year-old daughter and a two-year-old son.

One more thing to keep in mind: Change and compromise are completely different things. Change occurs 100 percent as a different action within oneself. Compromise is creating a different way to get to the same end. The compromise is about finding a different avenue to reach and to be agreed upon by multiple parties. There is a big difference between the two. It takes flexibility on at least two parties for compromise. Change is only about one person, and it comes from within.

Ten

If You're Not Feeling It in the First Five Dates

I cannot count how many times I've heard men and women in long-term relationships tell me that they knew it wouldn't work out from the start. And some of them, God bless their souls, are married or still currently in the relationship. They got into relationships that they now believe they can't get out of. But, it started off innocently enough. They thought they'd grow into the relationship. Or their partner would grow on them. Go figure. It just doesn't work that way. No matter how spectacular any individual is.

Unfortunately, some folks get to the point of desperation. And desperate isn't pretty on anyone. Desperation makes us do some pretty whacked-out things. Like get into something long term that isn't right on any level. In desperate times, we give up on those absolute needs and deal breakers to simply have a little bit of companionship. Then that companionship turns into loyalty, (which is admirable, but completely unnecessary) wherein one does not feel that they can leave. Eventually it comes around full circle, leaving you desperately seeking a way out.

If you're desperate, take a moment to look within and really find what is lacking in your life. Is it companionship, or is it fun? Or maybe it's humor? Or spontaneity? All these things can translate into desperation; however, a partner isn't necessarily a solution. You can take care of all these things on your own! Date yourself—spontaneously and without planning go to a funny movie and indulge in a private dinner before or after! You don't have to watch what you're eating as you can already love yourself! You have no one to impress!! Make yourself better by fulfilling your needs yourself, which will make you a better partner and more desirable!

I want to touch on the loyalty thing a bit more. Loyalty is an admirable trait. But it speaks far more about the person being loyal than the one the loyalty is toward. I've known so many people whose loyalty has become a deficit to their lives and, honestly, their character. No one will respect undue loyalty. Loyalty needs to be earned (beyond just being present) and returned. That applies to all relationships, not just romantic ones.

There's a reason why I feel that you should call it quits (if you haven't already) after five dates. I'm going to break it down for you.

The first date, if all goes well, is just what I like to call hearts and flowers. It doesn't have anything to do with the real you. I am not saying anyone is being fake, but we all want to make a great first impression. We are going to be watch our manners, language, and topic of conversation (often remaining quite superficial). It's been my observation that the only serious, real information that we get, from one another, at the first date is name and what we do (career, business, school, etc.). Outside of that, it's giggles and superfluous chatter. This is okay! And fun! Not to mention completely normal and exactly what should be brought to a first date.

Hopefully the first date went well, so it's on to the second date. This is where you actually get to see a little bit more into each other. But don't go too far. It's *only* the second date. Find out more about what each other does. Do they love their job? Hate it? Is their family close by? This is the time to find out some hobbies. It's all about the day-to-day of the person. Not the deep, dark skeletons. Those will come later. Still, this is time to keep things fluffy. You don't need to know their politics, blood type, or views on religion. And if last date was just a little coffee chitchat, let this one be longer and more personal. Lunch at minimum; dinner is even better.

Now the lovely third date is one of my favorites. You've found a little bit of comfort and gotten past the idiotic get-to-know-ya chatter. You're certainly invested in finding out more. And more means more. I've noticed personally and in speaking with people that the third date is what I refer to as the lust date. I know. It's kind of crass. But I call 'em like I see 'em. Although (and I know, this is completely gender biased) guys typically are good to go (read: sex) on any date, gals seem to have deemed the magical third date as the right time. Of course, everyone has their own rules, but it seems like the third date is the charm. Now, I don't endorse, suggest, push, or condone doing anything you aren't perfectly comfortable with at any time. This has just been my observation.

Here again, if you decide that third date is going to be the sex date, it's a major moment in the relationship going forward. And it's not about performance. It's about connection. This, physically, may not be as good as it's going to get, but you're on the verge. If you aren't making the physical connection (which has nothing to do with the ending, so to speak), think about where this relationship is going. As difficult and harsh as it may be, if the vibe isn't there, it's best to let things go and move on.

On the fourth date, you need to go there. What I mean by that is that if there are some skeletons in the closet lurking, you need to open up that door and shed some light on 'em. If you let things go farther than the fourth date (which, in reality could be still in the first week of meeting or could be a month out), you're going to insult the individual you're courting. At this point, you should start to evaluate how you feel about this new partner. If you think it could become serious then you need to be upfront and to the point. Before any deep, true feelings get involved, share those shadowy secrets that could, otherwise, negatively affect the relationship down the road. If they can't handle it in the honeymoon phase of dating, it's not going to get any better further down the line.

Fifth date: Make or break time. At this point you have seen, in part, the flirty self, the fun self, the sexy self, and the flawed self. By no means do you have 100 percent of any individual, but by the fifth date, you can make the call to stay or to go. You need to face a commitment or move on. Now, we all know that committed relationships can come and go. Commitment doesn't necessarily mean permanent, but the choice needs to be made. And yes, commitment does equal monogamy. You both have invested time, energy, effort, and emotion into each other. If you're not feeling it, let it go. Give someone else the chance. And I know I'm probably going to catch some letters/emails for this, but my policy: Even if it's a maybe after the fifth date, let it go. You may just need perspective as to what you actually want.

Don't agonize or elongate something that, really, doesn't have potential. And certainly don't just let it linger on until/if something better comes along. That's just selfish. Let the other party go on their merry way. Be honest.

Let them know that you are not feeling the connection that you had hoped for and that it is not a perfect fit for you. Own it. Be strong. Although the truth may hurt for a moment, in the long run, trying to make something work that ultimately is not, is going to be a lot more painful.

One last thought: If you find something within them that is a major, general, deal breaker (hygiene, racism, etc.), you may want to mention that to them upon letting go. Believe it or not, we sometimes don't see our own flaws. (Sarcasm.) We excuse ourselves and believe that if another is really worthy of our affection and love, they'll look past the issue.

Remember that being critical of others means that we need to be self-aware and look at our own personal issues from an honest and truthful perspective. As an example, being needy is a very common flaw. Needy can be perceived in many forms such as too much texting, too much calling, too many emails, too many demands of time, or constantly asking for attention or validation. I have had numerous clients who possessed this common flaw. I have always recommended that they try to allow their paramour to pursue them. Be more aloof and to try and make themselves less available.

Bringing a flaw to their attention may be a very useful bit of information for future romantic endeavors. But be kind, respectful, and as gentle as possible. This isn't a time to retaliate.

Part Two

You've Made It Past Five Dates, Now What?

Eleven

Commitment-Phobia

Is your significant other afraid to commit? Is he or she commitment-phobic? Have you been together two or three years or longer and your partner still won't fully commit? Then yes, your loved one might have commitment-phobia. But we are asked to understand and be forgiving of this particular issue because they need to work through some things, right? Nope. If they are truly, honestly diagnosed as commitment-phobic, they should be in therapy working on the issue, not lingering in a relationship. However, I have observed that many times when someone tells a romantic partner that they are having issues with commitment, they simply mean they don't want to commit to *you*. Move on. Don't delay your happiness with another by holding on to the idea of a life with someone who isn't in a place to fully engage in a relationship with the greatness that you have to offer.

You can easily tell if your significant other is commitment-phobic if he or she is unwilling to take the relationship to the next level or refuses to introduce you to family or friends. Or it can be as simple as when they self-identify as a commitment-phobe. When someone tells you they have never had a long-term relationship or are afraid of commitment, they are telling you they are commitment-phobic.

People become commitment-phobic for many reasons, but a couple of easy examples are that the person has been cheated on in the past or, sadly, some people are afraid to even have a successful relationship because they have never seen one in their own life.

Briefly I would like to point out a small misconception when it comes to so-called committed relationships. Many people equate marriage to commitment. Although marriage may be the ultimate sign of commitment, there are individuals who are perfectly happy with something less formal, and there is nothing wrong with that.

Obviously, there are various reasons to see a psychic with relationship questions. Just don't rule out your own, rational, logical self. A good psychic (it's too bad that there are some charlatans out there) will always tell you the straight dope—good, bad, or indifferent—regardless of what you may, or may not, want to hear.

Many times, I tune in to a relationship where my client needs to make an adjustment on their part. For example, changing their judgment or their perspective on how a past event occurred. Many times a man will do something to try to be protective that the gal interprets as controlling. When she can see the other side, it goes from irritating to endearing.

Twelve

Make Each Other Better

It seems like a pretty simple concept, right? When in a romantic relationship, it's best to make each other better. But this far outweighs honesty, respect, and loyalty. Those things are just good, solid foundations for any relationship, romantic or otherwise. Making each other better is about raising each other up in a deep, soulful, spiritual way. It's about bolstering one another to create not only the best relationship but the best individual each partner can be.

There are two schools of thought in relationship world. The first: you be the best you can be, putting yourself first, and by doing this, the entire relationship gets better. The second: the relationship needs to take precedence over everything else. If the relationship is in the best place, that creates happiness and harmony all around.

Let's discuss the first idea. If you put yourself first and make your happiness a priority, you're going to be in a better place for a relationship. Ultimately, your partner wants you to be engaged, attentive, and in love, so, if your mind is elsewhere (feeling unhappy or unfulfilled about something else lacking in your life), you can't be fully present in the relationship. Of course, the argument is where does putting you first end and selfish behavior begin. That's up to each individual.

A perfect example of this scenario is the workaholic. In this day and age, many of us define ourselves by our careers. We work twelve-hour days. We work from home. Weekends certainly aren't off-limits. We revel in the success coming from our ambition and determination. And *gasp* we actually find a great deal of happiness in our chosen occupation. Not to mention it often brings financial security, which makes us feel more comfortable in off-hours. Now, does the happiness we find in our career transcend to our romantic endeavors? Quite possibly. But is your partner willing to tolerate extended work hours? Maybe not, but the choice is yours.

Conversely, you may think it's best to put the needs of the relationship above your own. The idea is that the good for the many (both of you in the relationship) outweighs the few (just you). If you don't put the other person's expectations and needs before your own, it may be deemed selfish or self-involved. Unfortunately, sometimes, by doing this, you are putting your own needs and wants aside. By doing that, you could (but not necessarily) start to harbor resentment directed at your partner for not meeting your own relationship requirements.

It's incredibly important to speak your mind and get your voice heard in any relationship, romantic or otherwise! Not to mention to take time with your friends to give yourself some perspective and balance in your romantic relationship. When you do this, it only strengthens your relationship because you're gathering outside influences that will feed the romantic interests—not to mention gives you something to talk about over dinner! Outside influences are crucial! They give us perspective to develop our own thoughts and interests, which brings dimension to a relationship. Taking alone time can give you perspective to review your partner's behavior as well as your own, where you can then begin to gain clarity on situations within the partnership.

I do not believe there is a right or wrong path. What I do believe is this: I think every scenario and person needs to be looked at individually. What may work at one time may not the next due to emotion, time frames, determination, or whatever. So, with each situation that arises, look at it clearly, encourage input from your partner, and move in the direction that best suits you. Sometimes it may be that you need to follow your heart, regardless of concern communicated by your partner. Other times you just need to concede to their wants, knowing that at some point in the future all things will balance.

Let's speak to that balance. I don't believe in relationships being fifty-fifty 100 percent of the time. Just as life isn't always fair, relationships are not always in perfect harmony. Sometimes we need to carry one another. Whether that burden is financial, emotional, or practical, there is an ebb and flow to every relationship. If someone falls ill, we are going to want to take care of them and carry their burden (chores around the house, obligations, etc.). It's our nature. If someone loses a job and is temporarily stalled financially, we certainly don't immediately break up upon hearing the news. During these hard times, we want to carry the other to show our love and support. But it can't be that way full time.

For example, on January 18, 2013, I suffered a massive stroke and was hospitalized for four months. My husband Bobby was thrown into a situation where he had to be my advocate, my caretaker, my business manager, and my portal to the world. Not only did Bobby have to deal with doctors, nurses, and mountains of medical insurance, he had to cancel my scheduled appearances, answer emails, pay my bills, and cover my share of housekeeping duties. He fed me, clothed me, bathed me, and most importantly, sat at my bedside for weeks at a time just loving and comforting me; he was protector, my everything—and still is to this day.

The perfect balance, I believe, is semiconsistent imbalance. That sounds weird, doesn't it? But hear me out. I don't believe that every situation can be perfectly balanced. And we're constantly going through situations. One person has to lead, and one has to follow. Then, life changes and that leadership shifts. It's about the back and forth. And it's this leadership back and forth that shows the depth of each other's character, creating further respect and, ultimately, love.

Back in 1996 while I was in Wisconsin doing a radio appearance, Bobby and I were talking on the phone, and he was telling me he was not feeling well and experiencing an inordinate amount of anxiety and stress. He sounded so distressed that I chose to cut my trip short and rushed home that afternoon. I found him lying on the deck outside our townhouse, unable to function. Things became so bad that he was not able to return to work for six weeks. During that time, I had to call his employer daily, bring him to countless doctor appointments, get prescriptions filled, adjust his diet, administer medications, and much more. During all of this, he was barely able to get out of bed.

Something to remind yourself of here: Making each other better does not mean having the perfect relationship. In fact, it doesn't mean it's even good all the time. Let's face it. It's the tough moments that make us stronger and better as individuals. If we had it easy all the time, we'd just coast through life. But, fortunately (and even I can't believe I'm saying this), life brings us adversity to challenge us to rise to the occasion.

I'm going to get a little personal. My husband and I are opposites in a lot of ways—far too many to list, so you'll just have to take my word for it. Although we love each other dearly and are both committed to our marriage above all else, like any normal couple, we fight. And neither one of us were graced with those good arguing skills that every celebrity psychologist likes to tout. We're pretty typical. We'll name-call. We will certainly curse. But, in the thick of it, I noticed one thing: When I fight with my husband, I am more articulate, factual, and, in my opinion, witty than I am in a normal day. I share this because even in the worst of circumstances, he makes me a better person all-around—he makes me up my game. If I want to get my point across in conflict, I better articulate it pretty darn well. And that's my point. Making each other better doesn't always come in the best of moments.

On that note of having some challenging moments with our partners, I would say challenging one another is totally healthy and normal. It's okay not to buy into whatever your boy/girlfriend or spouse is passing along. In fact, you may find out more and further educate yourself if you choose to push back a little bit. No one likes a brown-noser, not for long, anyhow. We all like to have our intellect acknowledged, but it gets boring if you're with someone who is a doormat with no brain of their own. Be decisive. Speak your mind. Challenge a thought if you strongly disagree. Remember, we fall in love with the mind as much (if not more) as the heart.

In fact, challenges are exactly why opposites do attract. This is why a rugged, outdoorsy, lumberjack guy can find, and gain, interest from a glamorama, dolled up, girlie girl. But heed this warning: Although opposites attract, that attraction won't last long if you're not willing to take a chance and try something new! It's all about the balance. Sure, go out and find that polar opposite, but be willing and able to go out on a limb once in a while! Otherwise, that whole opposite thing isn't going to be engaging too terribly long.

Trying new things is just another way of lifting each other up. So what if your paramour is in love with horseback riding and you've never tried it. Do you know how awesome you're going to look just by giving it a whirl? (Not to mention it's a great reason for a new outfit.) And who knows? You may be the next world record equestrian. You just didn't know it. Countless couples I've talked with said they would have never tried something if their partner hadn't prompted them. And now, they find it's their favorite event/hobby. So put your great creative sense out there and share your passion with your new romance, but be willing to give their adventure a go as well!

On the flip side, there are people who bring out the worst in one another. Two people who have addictive tendencies or combative personalities may not be a great pairing. One couple I knew, a bartender and a heavy drinker, combined to make a cocktail of frequent and heated arguments. In the end, the breakup was nasty, to say the least.

Ironically, when she finally left the relationship, she took numerous bottles of valuable wine from his collection, which still bothers him to this day.

Thirteen

Romance, People!

Let's face it. Some of us are lacking in the romance department. For some, it's like a deficient gene in our DNA. It just isn't there. But here's the cool thing: It can be faked. Even if you don't have one romantic bone in your body, you can still be perceived as being romantic—maybe even a bit mushy. Although I hear about a lack more from the ladies, that doesn't mean that there aren't guys out there pining for their gals to step up the romance too. So let's talk about it. All hail the romance!

First, let us talk about what romance is and isn't. Romance isn't sex. In fact, it has nothing to do with sex. Of course, that could (and would for most) be the ultimate goal, but it really has nothing to do with sexual intercourse. Romance is the lovers' dance. It's the wooing of one another. It's showing your intentions, thoughts, and emotions in creative ways beyond the everyday spoken word (although writing a poem is extremely romantic, it's not something you'd do day-to-day). Although romance definitely involves doing special deeds, it's not about doing the deed.

It's about the ritual of love. Believe it or not, the idea of romance is relatively new. Not so long ago, most marriages were arranged. So wooing is kind of new. For many, the art of romance (and believe me, it's an art) is about courtship. A lot of folks would say it's the same thing, and to a degree it is. However, I believe you can court someone without being romantic. Romance is about the small things that you do for each other to remind your love of their place in your heart by giving them a token of your affection. Whether it's the grand gesture of flying your paramour off to Paris or simply picking a daisy while out on a walk (that last one always works for me), it's in that moment that you assure your partner that they are not only in your mind, but in your heart.

And to reinforce the idea that romance is in the heart, let me say this—romance isn't found in the wallet. Romantic moments have nothing to do with money. Not to say that you can't spend a few bucks working the love mojo, but it's not a requirement. In fact, when I mentioned I was working on this section of the book, I heard more stories about well-intentioned people going overboard on outlandish gifts when a handmade card would have worked.

Being showy isn't what romance is about. Save that for birthdays, holidays, and anniversaries. Romance is about those moments in-between where small, thoughtful gestures make the most impact. Allow me to share a story. Shortly after my husband and I got married, I found out that he loved, of all things, alphabet soup. So, I went and bought a couple cans on my next trip to the grocery store. At the time, I was in the corporate world and didn't come home for lunches, but he did. When I got home for the evening, I found, spelled out on my cutting board in alphabet soup letters, I LOVE YOU TIFFANY. Now tell me that is not romantic. Funny thing is, he had to open both cans to find all the letters. Needless to say, I had some leftover soup for dinner that evening. Bonus!

I think that unrealistic expectations keep a lot of people from even trying to dabble in romance. Think about the romcom (romantic comedy). Do those movies ruin it for us? God bless Hollywood. They have created an entire genre of movie entertainment specifically focused on the romantic notions and foibles of new, existing, and marital relationships. Here's the thing, folks, Hollywood is about exaggerating and dramatizing normal situations. It's entertainment. When you magnify typical situations, you inherently create humor and/or emotion. And it's not realistic to demand that kind of moment. Heck, just getting your hair right on a date can be a feat unto itself. But, it's not out of bounds to want or expect romance throughout your relationship.

Far too often I hear from individuals that although there was romance at first, it waned just a few short weeks into the endeavor. Remember, romance is about the conscious emotion made external. Just like appreciation (which romance most certainly includes), we can never be overappreciated. We can hear time and time again how much someone cares for us, and that, my friends, is what romance is about. Doing random things to show that love and caring. Why would anyone think that after a couple weeks, months, or years in a relationship that would get old? It never does.

Ladies, this applies to you too. I will admit the majority of people that I hear mentioning (read: complaining about) the lack of romance are women. There's no question. However, it doesn't mean that the dudes are not looking to pump up the romance in their lives. They are! I hear more every day from men who are reaching out, trying to be romantic and thoughtful with playful or protective gestures, but their gals are shutting them and the opportunity down. What a loss. And remember that romance is a two-way street. Although guys may not be as responsive to things like flowers (note: I know a ton of guys who really like 'em), teddy bears, and chocolate, they do love a massage, their favorite beer icy cold in the fridge, and taking time for you to engage in their favorite hobby. It works both ways.

One sure-fire romantic element (outside of a specific example): Surprise. A surprise is integral to romance. It's out of the blue. It's not an agreed upon destination/

experience/thing. It's something that is created or planned by one individual to show the other the place in the heart that they hold. Without the element of surprise, you're going to deflate the romance.

None of us are getting any younger (and if you are, email me immediately). In that vein, the idea of what romance is will change over time. Heck, when I was twenty-one, I thought the boys buying my shots at the bar were pretty romantic. Not to say that buying someone drinks isn't a thoughtful gesture, but is that still in my romance definition? No. I've grown up a bit. At this point in my life, dual, personal experiences are much more romantic to me than anything else. Say, for example, a wine tasting. But for you and your situation, your love may just be looking for a handwritten note telling them of your feelings. Or maybe it's holding their hand on a walk when you typically aren't an outwardly affectionate person. But, whatever it is, don't expect the same things to work for the next several years. Change it up. Our tastes and feelings toward most everything change as we do. Romance is no different.

And then there are kids. I cannot tell you how much your idea of romance will change after children come in the picture. Although I don't, personally, have children, I certainly hear about the change of life after the blessed birth. There is no question that kids enhance the lives of their parents. However, the time and effort it takes to raise a child encroaches on any time you may have for those special romantic moments. So, with children, our perception and ideas of romance change as well. Instead of a candlelit dinner, it may just be having an hour to yourself to read a book or take a bubble bath. The bottom line is that although children enter the relationship, there is no need to eliminate or put less importance on romance.

Let's talk a little bit about what romance isn't. Now, of course, what romance is and is not is entirely personal and varies from one individual to another. However, I'm fortunate enough to talk to a lot of folks about pretty personal stuff and I can tell you this: Practical items are not romantic. We all get it. We need things like dishwashers and tires. But let's not turn them into the surprise gift. Although we can appreciate things like central air conditioning and coffee makers, these things don't say what is in the heart—they say clean my house and get me to the mall. Tread lightly with these things when presenting them as romantic gifts.

I will leave you with some very simple things/ideas that you can do to show your love to that someone special in your life.

- Love notes and cards
- Drawing a bath
- Reminding them of a special date or action they did that you remember fondly
- Sometimes lighting a candle is all it takes
- Buy them their favorite foods

- Take them on a surprise date
- Offer them a massage
- Do a chore that they do not want to do

Have you held hands lately while walking? Just hold your partner's hand, even if it's just sitting on the couch while watching TV.

Fourteen

Moving In Together

Alright, you made the commitment. You're totally in. You actually like this person enough to share space. But do you do it? Do you take the plunge? Cohabitation is a big thing. You aren't just taking the relationship to the next level, you're intertwining lives. Not to mention finances, schedules, and other miscellaneous stuff. But is it really a good idea?

Let's just hit the big dog right up front. The idea of living together before marriage makes some people a little edgy. The reason? Religion. Dogmatic Christian religious doctrine tells us this isn't a good idea for the individual to live in sin (hence the term). But let's face it, we can excuse a lot of things that seemingly go against the Bible. Swearing and lust are examples. None of it is encouraged by Christianity as a whole. Can we rest assured that 90 percent of America takes part in those activities? Yes, I think we can. But, in a different day and time, things were perceived differently. And we might have family members of a different generation. You have to make it right, within you, if you want to walk down the living-together road. You may have to answer some pretty tough questions not only about the significant other, but your morality. Be prepared.

And speaking of those little things we call morals and ethics, ask yourself this question: Is moving in together outside of marriage fundamentally part of who you are? Consider where you stand personally, morally, and ethically on the subject. It defines you, not only to friends and family, but also to a potential partner. All religion aside, people have severe and specific opinions on the topic. And you may very well feel that you have to defend your position. For many individuals, it's a hot topic and quite controversial. As much as we all have opinions on everything from diet to politics, this is one of those touchy topics that could define you regardless of what stance you take. So take it seriously and make sure your position jibes with who you are and what you are all about.

Statistics indicate that 70 percent of couples cohabitate before marriage. So the idea isn't really unique or out of the mainstream, and by no means is it taboo. However, another little factoid to mull over is that, by the same study, of those who live together, 85 percent of the couples break up. So, facts tell us that a higher percentage of relationships don't make it if they live together prior to marriage. Does that make you stop and think? That is your call. Most people, when you talk to those who are pro-moving-in, say that they move in specifically to avoid the down-the-road breakup and all the associated heartache. Others, the more conservative folks, don't endorse the idea of living together prior to marriage because all the magic and newness of discovering one another after marriage is then gone. You have been playing house for a time without the higher level of commitment. Both sides have good arguments.

If you're serious about moving in, why not marry? If you really believe that your relationship has staying power, isn't moving in together just the weigh station to marriage? For some (and I would venture to say most), yes; for others, no. They take it a bit more nonchalantly. In this day and age, we are waiting longer to marry and take that final step. And there are lots of reasons, the biggest of which, again, is monetary. Since we're waiting longer to get married, some individuals are creating financial issues that aren't the best to marry into. The economic turmoil has affected everyone, including eligible singles. So, moving in may be the solution to those wanting to marry, but feeling it's not the best call to protect oneself. For those who take more of a cavalier attitude about moving in, the idea may center on money as well. It's easy to understand; it's simply cheaper to live with someone than to live alone. You can save more sharing expenses, housing costs, and so forth.

If you choose to move in and take the romance to the next level, you may want to check out whether or not your community recognizes common-law marriages. Common-law marriages exist all over the world, not just in the United States. These laws do have several, typically simple, requirements. You typically have to be over the age of majority (usually eighteen years old, but it varies from state to state); live together for a certain amount of time, and project yourself as a married couple. If you are in a state/community that recognizes a common-law marriage, you have all the benefits as well as all the intricacies of a traditional marriage. One huge example: in states with common-law marriage, the Internal Revenue Service allows you to file taxes as married, filing separately. However, one more thing to ponder—there is no such thing as a common-law divorce, still making the breakup, if it comes to that, quite difficult.

With the combining of living space often comes the purchase of mutual goods. Furniture, food, toiletries, extending all the way to pets may be joint purchases. Much like moving in together, this is just another step to deepen the connection to one another. I know I'm going to sound like a downer, but another piece to consider is: If this relationship doesn't work out, how do you split up those items? Things can be split up, but when a relationship goes south, often, so does the civility. You can't cut a couch in half. And goodness knows you can't split up a pet. How will you divide the assets in the case of dissolution? My suggestion is to talk about the what-ifs up front so all things are understood and predetermined far ahead of anything detrimental happening.

When is the right time to move in together? Again, that can only be determined by you and your partner. For some, it's a matter of months, for others, it's years. Unfortunately, one person may be ready a lot sooner than the other.

Here are a couple examples of couples who have moved in together and the relationships have either flourished or floundered.

I knew a guy and gal just out of high school who were both nineteen years old. Neither had lived away from their parents, and they were not planning on heading off to college. They were in love and decided to get jobs, find an apartment, and grow old together. So they saved up a few bucks and got a place. Within days they realized they had made a mistake. They may have dated for a long time, but they never really saw how each other lived inside their parents' home. They agreed on almost nothing, like how the furniture should be arranged, how much time their friends would spend hanging out in the apartment (and getting in the way), and even little things about whether leaving the television on at night was acceptable or not. Needless to say, after just two months, they broke up. The girl moved back home with her parents, and the boy had to find a new roommate to complete the lease agreement. The couple never spoke to each other again. Both now realize they really never had much in common with one another to begin with, and this was because they simply didn't know.

A much more positive story is actually about two different couples who made very successful transitions moving in with one another. Why were they both so successful? I'll tell you. See the two girls lived together in their own apartment, attending community college and getting by in life just fine. Their two boyfriends lived in town, one had his own place and the other was still at home with mom and dad. Obviously, the boys would spend a lot of time at the girls' apartment. One of the boys was kind of a neat freak, but he never complained about the dirty and unorganized bathroom. He simply cleaned it. No complaints, no bitching—he just got it done. He was also never shy about breaking out the vacuum and also making sure the sink was free of dirty dishes. The other boy liked to cook, and he always seemed to be bringing over the groceries and cooking for everyone. These four people spent about a year together in that apartment getting to know one another, even sitting down at the table and enjoying supper together, just like they did growing up at home. They would talk about all sorts of stuff and got to know most everything about each other. They worked through their differences over a period of time. Sure, there were a few disagreements, but most of those were what they were going to watch on TV or what club they were going to party at on the weekend, so nothing too major. Well, after about a year, it was time to move and go their separate ways. Each couple went off and got their own apartment. None of these four people had ever lived with just their girlfriend or boyfriend but the outcome was very successful. Both couples got married within a year and to this day, twenty years later, both couples are happily married, with homes and families. This would have not been the likely outcome had they not spent all that time getting to know each other so well, learning about the little things that can nag at you and drive a wedge into a relationship. A very small thorn can grow into a very infected wound, but these folks had removed those tiny thorns from their relationships. They had already seen the good, the bad, and the ugly before they set off on their own to make lives together.

The question will always remain whether a couple should live together before marriage. Sometimes families get in the way by suggesting that living in sin is not something they can support, but I say go for it. I believe most couples should absolutely live together before getting married. I've seen too many marriages fall apart and most of them were not built on a healthy foundation. They have the same problems as the nineteen-year-olds in my first story; they didn't know enough about each other, and then all of a sudden they get married and move in together. It's not always a recipe for disaster, oftentimes it works, but when it goes bad, it goes very bad, and what comes next is heartbreaking. There is divorce, the separation of assets, and of course the big one, if they do have kids, is child support and visitation. For the next two decades, these two people must continue to interact with one another for the good of the children, but in truth they really don't like each other anymore. Those are long and painful years for those folks, and it all could have been avoided had they lived together first before getting married. Some people may read this and state that I am suggesting couples should live in sin before marriage. I don't really look at it that way, but yes I would recommend it.

Regardless, don't let anyone guide you. You have to do what feels right for you and your relationship. Always a psychic, whether it's a client or a friend, I consistently recommend following your gut. Whatever your intuition tells you is most likely exactly what needs to happen. And surprisingly, your intuition will guide you regardless of what your heart says. I can't tell you how many times I've heard, "My heart tells me one thing but my gut tells me another." Go with the gut 100 percent of the time. It won't ever lead you astray.

Finally, don't move in unless you can really, truly see yourself marrying this individual. If you have decided that, on all levels, moving in is where you want to be, know that marriage needs to be (fingers crossed) the ultimate goal and result to the cohabitation. Although the monetary benefits are tempting otherwise, it's not fair to the other person if you're not willing to seriously go there in your head and in your heart, about marriage. If you don't see this person as a potential lifelong partner, don't sign the lease.

Fifteen

Privacy

Boy oh boy. Privacy can be a major point of contention in any relationship. Frequently we hear about our right to privacy in the workplace. But these days we're also talking about privacy in personal relationships. The big question that I hear from clients is: What is the difference between secret and private? It's a pretty smart question. Although I don't believe there is an absolute answer for anyone, I'll share what I've learned, seen, and heard. Hopefully, at a minimum, that'll give you a baseline. As the definition of love is different for every person, so is the idea of privacy.

The first issue that we should tackle is if anything is really private in relationships. Is privacy required? Is privacy a right despite your partnership and commitment? Obviously the idea of privacy, much like respect, should be a situation that is earned. If someone steps out of bounds (read: has an affair), you have a right to be cautious and questioning. But let's leave that out of the discussion, at least for now. What I have found to be a good rule of thumb is this: If you feel that you have to hide something from your partner, chances are it's not a privacy issue, but more of a moral/ethical relationship issue. If there is embarrassment or shame, know that you've probably done something wrong to warrant that feeling and don't do it again. However, if you are only doing something to retain your identity as an individual, that, dear reader, is another issue. Let's say there is agreement that you each keep your financial stuff separate. Are you required, if asked, to reveal what you've agreed to keep individualized? No. You're not. It's private. You set that precedent. However, taking out a credit card in your spouse's name, charging it up, and then having your spouse discover it? Well that's just secretive, and, frankly, underhanded. Hopefully you can see the difference. Private is fine. Secretive is inherently bad.

Another factor in the privacy game is this: relationship length. Let's keep using financial scenarios as our example. I don't think that it would be uncommon after several dates to reveal your income level. That's a private thing, but you're probably not being subpoenaed for the information. However, sharing intimate details of your financial standing after knowing someone a couple of days would never be expected. Now let's say you are seeing each other for several months. Things are moving along and the relationship is deepening. You two talk about moving in together. Is there a right to know more about your partner's financial situation? Sure! By cohabitating through buying a house or renting an apartment together, they are essentially joining your credit rating. The choices that one makes affect the other. It's as simple as that. In that scenario, if you move in together and, maybe, um forget (hope you're picking up on the sarcasm) to mention your looming $50,000 student loan debt, well that's just being secretive and misleading. You have committed to this person. You need to expect to be upfront and straightforward with what is real and honest. Here again (and yes, I'll keep saying this), if there is something shameful about what you have done, you are being secretive and not private.

I think it is entirely human, with or without cause, to want to snoop, poke, and prod around in your lover's business. Heck, we love and care about them—we want to know more. That's fair. But ask. Don't dig. There's no need. If you have a healthy, open relationship, push back those basic desires (we do it all the time by passing on the second piece of pie) and take the high ground. There, truly, is nothing to be gained by going where you shouldn't. Because, what if you, Lord forbid, find something? How do you bring that up? How do you justify your actions? You sunk, exactly, to the level of the person hiding the information. If you have questions about your partner, the first, second, and third rule is to communicate. If you really question your partner, or seriously doubt that communicating will do any good, then maybe you should, instead of looking to find evidence to prove your point, simply leave the relationship. There is something much deeper going on than just your curiosity. Admit to yourself that you are the one with the trust issues and should find a different situation that better suits your relationship needs.

More specifically, let's discuss phone records. Oh, our lovely smartphones now offer so much more than just a simple phone. They are our phone, email, camera, and god forbid, our video recorder (not to mention texting and instant messaging). They can record where we have been (GPS) and who we are with (thanks to all of the check-ins on social media outlets). Although we use them for personal things, oftentimes we also use them for various professional reasons. The reason I bring this up is that I cannot tell you how many times I have heard from the frantic client questioning the phone numbers and texts when they have gone a-snoopin'. Let's go there again: Don't go looking for trouble. If the phone in question is utilized for professional use, give all uncertain information the benefit of the doubt. But know this—you shouldn't be looking there anyway!

I received a phone call from client who was freaking out because she had gone through her husband's phone and found a contact for "wife." Of course, she was terribly upset when she saw that the number listed was not her own. When I tuned in to this situation, I saw that it was just a nickname for a co-worker he spent a lot of time with—his "work wife." The listing in his phone meant no disrespect to my client, and she unfortunately had overreacted to something that was obviously not clear. Once she realized her misunderstanding, she was able to go to her husband and express her displeasure with the nickname/terminology he had used as a contact in his phone. Her husband completely understood her displeasure, apologized, and immediately changed the contact name in his cell phone. Fortunately, this misunderstanding, which could have escalated into something dire such as a divorce or separation, did not, thanks to my reading and her presence of mind to call and get some clarity.

Here is the moral of this entire story: Stay out of people's private business. Make decisions on what is and what is not considered private in your relationship. There isn't anything wrong with someone wanting to retain their own, personal identity within a couple. But make those boundaries known to each other. And for God's sake, adhere to them. Honestly, honoring the personal nature of each other only strengthens the bond between you two. If you go looking for something that is nefarious and questionable, you are no better than the person secretively hiding it in the first place. Be open. If you question something be an adult and ask. If you don't like the answer, then you always have the choice to move out of the relationship and find exactly what you need.

Sixteen

Me Time

What is me time? It's that time set aside just for you, to spend with only you, and you alone. Whether it's reading a book, staring out a window, taking a hike, or meandering at the mall, it's solely your decision. That's what makes it special. It is time for you and for your thoughts. Unfortunately, with everyone being ridiculously interconnected via social media and wireless technology, we don't get enough of it. And, more importantly and unfortunately, we tend to either lose sight of it or make it less of a priority when getting involved in an important relationship.

Especially in the beginning of a relationship, we get caught up in our time or us time. Me timc goes right out the window. But silly us, we forget that it was that me time that really identified us as individuals and made us attractive to our new, potential partner. Time together is great; it is wonderful and can be magical. It is what drives the relationship and creates a bond. Time together is truly a blessing. But, don't allow all that our time to completely replace your own personal activities that make you, YOU. Our time needs to benefit you both. That's what it is about. Unfortunately, too many folks get so wrapped up in pleasing each other that they fail to take time to make number one (you) happy!

And that leads me to another point. Far too frequently we believe that putting another before ourselves is the intensely selfless maneuver. Outside of a parent-child relationship, I beg to differ. Being the people-pleaser is in my estimation and humble opinion, totally selfish. Yes, I said selfish. How you ask? Here's why: When you constantly defer to another's whim, will, or decision, you never have to take any accountability for your own life. This only creates a victimization role for the people-pleaser. If things go wrong, well, you just followed the pack and did what someone else decided. If things go right, you humbly bow your head as part of the team and go to great lengths to let people know that you just wanted to be there, help, or take care of the other. Here's the thing… People-pleasers don't come from a place of wanting to do good. They want to be nice. Goodness is an inherent trait within someone. Being nice is a decision how to act. And we all know that doing what is good and right isn't always being nice.

Your time is your time to process what you need to—outside of the relationship. Although we love and hopefully respect our partner's opinions, ultimately our way of coming to conclusions is wholly our own. We learn on our own time in our own way. As such, we need that personal time to work through the multitude of issues that we run into each and every day. However, your time does not necessarily need to be spent in deep, personal thought. It could simply be time to do something inane or completely selfish for yourself. You could use me time to run out and have Indian food if your companion doesn't care for that type of cuisine. Just because they don't care for it doesn't mean that you should sacrifice something that you love. Or maybe you are a big sports nut. Your time can consist of playing or watching the sport. Taking the time to reinforce who and what you are and what you're about only serves to better the relationship.

Working on and taking time for you can only benefit the relationship. I can't stress that enough. Think about it: When you stop taking the time for those things that you know and love, you start resenting what is occupying that time—your new partner. Relationships are meant to bolster and better the individual while creating a unified bond. If you start taking away those things that, ultimately, make you who you are, you're only going to create a wedge between yourself and the one that you are trying to grow with.

Spending time alone will only strengthen and improve your relationship. I will use myself and husband as an example (again). We spend a lot of time together; we are best friends and, for the most part, share common interests. However we both agree that being around each other 24/7 for weeks on end can be a bit grueling. When we get to this point, we know that we are overdue to get some me time. My personal preference is to go out with one of my girlfriends to have lunch, maybe a cocktail, and then go shop, shop, shop! When I come home and see my husband, I am refreshed and excited to tell him about my day and show off all my new clothes and shoes. My husband tends to create a little me time late in the evenings or sometimes small little breaks during the day on the weekends. His vice is video games, in particular, what seems to be the only game people play nowadays: Call of Duty on Xbox. When he is feeling stressed or just needs a break from me or a break from the day, he goes downstairs, fires up the game console and the big screen TV, and starts "blowing shit up" (his words, not mine). After a couple of hours, he comes back up a whole new guy and wants nothing more than to spend the next part of his day with me.

Far, far too often, people, especially women (I know, saying this is gender biased, but it's been my observation), feel that being alone equates to being lonely. Unfortunately, this frequently comes from a point in time when they felt lonely because they were without a mate, and now they assume the same feeling whenever they are alone. It's not the case. Don't fear being alone. Being alone gives you the time to let you be you without demands. It's only in this time, without the day-to-day bombardment of the world, that we can really see what we feel and need. Just think of how much you process while driving! We all have had experiences where we got in our car, drove to our destination, and were completely clueless how we got there! That's processing! It's letting your mind wind out to form opinions, thoughts, upcoming actions, and all of the other good stuff. Make sure to give yourself that time without fear.

You have hobbies. Your partner has hobbies. Just because you both love to share time together doesn't mean that you have to embrace each others' outside passions. My husband is an amazing fisherman. He's been fishing since he was a young boy. I appreciate that. I get it. Goodness knows that I love nature. However, is my version of nature his version? Nope. I'd rather sit out in the sun and read a book. He'd rather throw baits. Does this make either of us bad people? Of course not. It's great when hobbies and interests are mutual. But don't force it. Guilting anyone to do anything that isn't of interest just creates a wedge between the two. A solution: find something else, above and beyond your individual hobbies, that the two of you can enjoy as a couple and make it your activity.

I know I mentioned it earlier, but I'm really going to continue to stress it. What drives a relationship is the uniqueness of each other. It just can't be said enough. It's one thing to be complete opposites who have differences at every turn. But, let's face it. If that were the case, the relationship would never get off the ground. Taking time, separately, only works to better the relationship. Remember, there's a reason for the old adage, "Absence makes the heart grow fonder." It's true! If you and your partner are together every moment of every day, assuming that you'll have the rest of your lives together, how boring and, frankly, tedious, does that sound? Never having a different experience beyond the relationship to share? Nothing new to bring to the dinner table for discussion creates some long, boring meals.

Many, many couples have decided that boys' nights out/girls' nights out are a way to work on individual needs. I think they're a great idea if that's what you really feel is lacking. Do I think that is the only solution? I don't. Although hanging out with friends is great and something we all need (social interaction piece), do I really believe that within that time that we process our deeper thoughts? No. Social interaction isn't the solution to really taking time to do as you and only you would do. Friends, albeit fun, are more distraction and/or an addition to the busy mind rather than time to clear out and process.

This is my extra special note to all the young men and women out there: Although it sounds ageist, remember, as you read this section, I've been there, looking for the One and fawning over a new paramour. I've been the silly girl swooning and sometimes shedding tears over some new boy that had come into my life. Okay. All that being said, I'm going to sound like an old woman saying this: If I only knew then what I knew now. Kids, don't live your life for that next phone call, text, or instant message. Anticipation is just fine. But value your time. Don't sit around, stalling out your life, waiting for someone to give you three minutes of their time whenever it suits them. Live. If you're not there to respond to their message, so what? Life goes on. It shows them that you have a life, and I promise they'll be there when you get back. And if they called you once, missing you, they'll call again. Your time is just as precious as theirs and anyone else. The chase, for boys and girls alike, is part of the fun. Enjoy it. I promise, guarantee (and that's not a word I take lightly), and swear that taking my advice won't steer you wrong.

Seventeen

Long-Distance Relationships

Oh, the long-distance relationship. The stuff that sappy, chick flick, cable-network movies are made of. What happens when we find Mr. or Ms. Right and they don't live down the block? Do we make it work? Do we have the commitment level it's going to take to create a fruitful relationship? Heck, for some it's a simple question of keeping our hands to ourselves and remaining faithful. For others, it's a bit more complicated. Let's talk about it.

In a perfect world, we meet other singles in our close geographic area. For most, this works best. Whether it's at the grocery store, church, bar, or through mutual acquaintances, we typically find love close by. From there we can create and foster a more traditional courting scenario. We see each other on a regular basis and, after a bit of time, decide if we want to deepen the relationship. However, the world we live in is a changing. Dating has not only become national, but international.

Just a few decades ago, air travel was an extreme luxury. And just a few years ago, we had to pay long-distance to call fifty miles down the road, but now technology has completely revolutionized the world of dating and relationships. Now, with the Internet and the invention of social media, we can talk to and meet people all around the planet. We don't necessarily need to be confined to individuals hanging around our own neighborhood. Not only can we communicate, but we can see them through video chat. Which brings a whole new dimension to the singles' scene.

Dates and dating no longer have to be in person, face-to-face. Wherever our laptop can go, so can our potential mate. If there is a Wi-Fi connection to be had, there can be that immediate interaction. I've seen people schedule virtual dates for various activities. Watching a movie on the couch? Why not put it on in both homes and watch it together while chatting on the Web? Want to go out for a drink or cup of coffee? Bring the laptop and do that together. Heck, the advent of Internet bars are based around that exact idea. We teleconference all the time in corporate world, why not tele-date?

And the idea of a shared experience via technology doesn't stop there. Yes, you know where I'm going—phone sex. Or video chat sex. It seems like there should be some nifty slang term for that, but there isn't. I checked. Heck, even sexting is not only viable, but frequently in the news thanks to unfaithful celebrities. Phone sex (I'm going to use that as the generic term, from here on out for all of the above), for those in a long-distance relationship, can really help to complete the bond of a relationship without the true physical intimacy. Here again, you're sharing an experience that is entirely personal and showing vulnerability by doing so. Hence, the end result is a deeper connection. Although this may not be the ideal—isn't that the theme for long-distance relationships—it's a good substitute. Anyone you talk to that is in a long-distance relationship will tell you that this piece is integral to staying together long term.

Another key factor to the long-distance relationship: trust. No matter how much we are infatuated with another, distance can create trust issues. We can be the most loyal, trusting individual, but given some time of not communicating in a way we deem fit, and the monster that is mistrust can creep in. Regardless of our past experiences, cheating or not, we can find ourselves letting those thoughts of infidelity rent a billboard in our head. Although absence may make the heart grow fonder, it also allows the mind to create subpar scenarios. The only way around this is communication, communication, communication.

As I mentioned while discussing tele-dating and phone sex, it's about the shared experience. Communication is sharing one's life through your own perceptions. If you are going to commit to the long-distance relationship, you must make communication a paramount priority. It doesn't matter if you are a communication expert or a shy, introverted soul. Your own personal comfort level needs to be put aside and the communication aspect of the relationship needs to come to the forefront. The basis of any long-term, romantic relationship is based in the mind. And communication is how minds connect. If there is no communication, the relationship won't endure. It's that simple.

Something else to ponder about the long-distance relationship: Is this a temporary or permanent situation? When a new relationship starts to blossom, we want to be with each other all the time. That's the beauty of a new commitment. But, of course, we all need to get into the relationship to see how things go. Big decisions don't need to be and shouldn't be made in haste. However, with time, we fall more into a pattern, and we must discuss whether or not the travel back and forth is going to continue. So wait a few weeks or a couple months, but do have that discussion. How is it going to work? Are you going to take turns traveling back and forth? How does it fit into each other's schedule? Once you establish the how to, next on the agenda needs to be the permanency.

So, all goes well and you shuttle back and forth. The long-distance thing agrees with you both and the relationship continues to grow and mature. Great! But then one thing leads to another. Talk of the big M comes up. Yes, marriage. This is great. It's a natural and logical progression, and exciting too! But now you need to think even more long term. Who moves? Now, some folks conclude that even though they want to make the ultimate commitment, they don't need to physically be in the same place. However, most people want to share a home with their partner. So, for those who have a more traditional viewpoint on marriage and cohabitation, the discussion needs to be had of who is going to move where. Now, there may be an obvious answer. One's home may be much bigger or more accommodating. There may be children involved. Outside of those things, if housing, finances, and jobs are equal, how do you make that decision?

Ultimately, who moves where is up to the couple. There isn't a right or wrong way of making that decision. It could be as simple as one simply being more willing. Or the economic market being better to sell/lease in a community. Maybe the cost of living is lower in one area than another. All these things need to be considered when making the transition. The best suggestion I can make is probably the most obvious: Make a pro/con list. Let the facts decide if the two of you can't make a clear decision.

Although the long-distance relationship probably isn't the optimum solution for most, it can be done. Case in point: military families. It's a mega-bummer when someone has to be shipped away, oftentimes overseas. However proud you are to be serving your country or to be part of a partnership with a soldier, it still is very hard to be apart from your loved one. Now, the argument may be that this situation is unique, but the fact remains that it's two people, committed, apart from one another. However honorable the situation may be, these individuals still have to adapt. They are susceptible to all the same circumstances that any other long-distance couple face, maybe even more so.

Unfortunately, it's been my observance that many have tried the long-distance relationship, but few have succeeded.

Here are two quick stories about long-distance relationships, one that worked and one that failed miserably.

I met a couple at a paranormal convention a few years back. Oddly enough, they met each other at a similar event the previous year. I didn't know it at the time, but one lived in Tennessee and the other in Kentucky. From what I could tell, these two were married, living together in a home somewhere, and making it happen. I was a little floored to find out they lived so far apart. Of course, they were talking about closing the gap and trying to decide which one would have to move, but they were still very happy and committed with the current setup. Both had long-term jobs and mortgages. Change like that requires a great deal of time and planning, but it seemed like they were eventually planning on living together. They saw each other at least every month or month and half, they traveled to paranormal events throughout the year, sharing hotel rooms and meals, creating lots of fun, enjoyable memories. When they eventually decided to make the leap, it was the man who decided to pick up his life, leave his job, sell his home, and move to another state, all to be with his girl. Their first year was a little rough, as you could imagine. There was a job change and a decision on whose furniture would stay in the house or get stored, among other considerations, but they had exceptional communication and were very understanding of one another. They effortlessly found compromise on all things big and small. Now, four years later, they are married and still living in the woman's home, though both names are now on the mortgage. I see them growing old together. They are a very happy couple who paid their dues in a long-distance relationship that ended up working.

My next story of a long-distance relationship did not end up as well. This one is pretty short and typical. A girlfriend from here in the Midwest met a boy at college who lived down in Arizona. They saw each other as often as possible, but there were the expected trust issues in play. They would fight over things like why the boy didn't text her last night after she knew he was going out on the town with his buddies. She loved him but also wanted to trust him and believe in what he had been telling her. Well, the day came when she and her family had to go down to Arizona, but she didn't mention this to her boyfriend. She just figured that the boy loved her and would thoroughly enjoy the pop-in visit. She couldn't have been more wrong. When she got to Arizona, she took her parents' rental car and drove to see her boyfriend, but when she arrived, she found one little problem. The boyfriend answered the door and immediately came outside to speak to her, not allowing her in the house. At this point, he confessed that he was actually married, had a young daughter, and his wife was pregnant with their second child. He begged this girl to not make a scene and asked her to please just leave, closing with "I will explain it all later"—so she left and never spoke another word to him again. Her heart was broken, and still is. She now has serious trust issues and finds it hard to have successful relationships with men.

I didn't share this last story to scare you. The last thing I want to do is discourage anyone. However, I do believe in understanding the facts. Dating but living apart from those we love is difficult. It takes a great deal of commitment and a strong will to make these types of relationships last for the long haul. Although I believe long-distance relationships can work, it takes a special kind of couple to really make it work. But, for those that do, it seems like an unbreakable bond. It really makes the couple stronger. They come from a place of honoring and respecting one another that you may not see in a more traditional couple. Those couples really know how to make that time with each other, as precious as it is, special. And that's something we could all learn from.

Eighteen

Love Isn't All You Need

Now I don't mean to take the wind out of your sails, because I'm all about the romance . . . but I'm even more about the real. Love is grand and love is divine, but the reality is that love, albeit amazing, does not pay the rent, or the grocery bill, or the utilities. Granted, love is the stuff that gets you through tough times in relationships, but there is just so much more to it.

Beyond love comes listening. Frankly, if you ask any gal out there, she'll tell you that her love came from listening. Girls fall in love between the ears, boys. It's true. It's all about what we hear from each other. But, beyond that initial phase, it's listening to each other's thoughts, ideas, dreams, and goals because from that, you are going to learn their likes and dislikes, and the reasons behind each.

If you can learn to listen and really hear what they have to say, you'll have a fruitful and long relationship. The biggest gripe I hear from both genders when speaking to people in long-term relationships, is not "they don't love me," but "they don't hear me." This is so sad, but all too often, so true. The reason listening is so important is because every issue in a relationship is affected by communication.

Take money, the most dreaded M word, for example. Every statistic shows, when it comes to marriages breaking up, 90 percent of the time it is money related. So, you may be able to live on love, but it sure doesn't keep food in the belly, which is pretty darn essential. Now, money is not the only factor in a marriage, but having financial issues will drive those other cracks open like nothing else. They can make a marriage raw. Let's get real for a second. I do not believe that money is the source of happiness nor do I think it is the root of all evil. I do believe that money simply equals freedom. Money can give you the time and space to do pleasurable things and to avoid things that you would rather not do. Could you grow and raise your own food? Sure. Could you go chop wood to heat your home when needed? Probably. Do you want to? Probably not. We've become accustomed to having those things taken care of for us by another, for a price.

Because money gives us time and freedom, monetary problems invade the fun time that you can have with your partner. And not having time with each other, quickly and simply, breaks down the relationship. Now, do we need to be filthy rich? No. But, our standard of living needs to be agreed upon between the two involved in the relationship. Although that sounds very business oriented, it does help build relationships and common goals. If your vision of wealth and security differs from your partner, you're going to have a conflict no matter how much love exists.

And then there is family. Watch any exploitative talk show and before long you'll see that extended family can, and will, influence a relationship. Although you may love one single member of the family, we all need to understand that we are a package deal. No matter what our relationship is with those outside family members, we are connected to them. Sometimes, if you're lucky, it really works out well and you love the extended family as much as you love the individual. However, for many of us, the parents, siblings, and extended kin are a little rough around the edges.

Warning: although I completely and totally believe that a family should speak their mind and share their thoughts, being in a relationship with someone who takes family opinion over their own is a major red flag. Sure, considering the opinions of others is a good thing. I believe in consensus. And sometimes, when involved in a romantic relationship, we overlook precarious situations that others can see more clearly. However, when your suitor acts, reacts, or behaves per the family wishes, steer clear. This is a sign of someone who will never make a decision, never take charge, and as a result, never accept responsibility. Every conflict the couple has (and there are always issues) will end up involving the extended family. And no one needs that. Unfortunately, it's an issue that rarely gets resolved.

If issues with extended family don't scare you off, the next huge issue is the prospect of extending your future family. In other words, let's discuss kids. Pretty early on, potential mates should know where they stand on the idea of having children. And, if you don't see eye-to-eye in that department, it's a deal breaker (see Deal Breakers, chapter 4). But, beyond just the idea of conception, how are you going to choose to raise those kids? Believe it or not, in my practice, a top-five hurt in relationships is differences in how to not only discipline, but school, feed, and spiritually guide children. Some folks believe in tough love. Some believe in corporal punishment. Others believe that children should be allowed to express themselves however necessary. There are those who believe that academics aren't as important as creativity. Where this really breaks down a marriage is on the teamwork front. If little Johnny knows that he can go to one parent for something that the other didn't allow, you don't exactly have a unified front. And isn't that what marriage is all about? That unified partnership? Here again, you can love each other endlessly, but how to pass along that love to something created by each one of you may be a different distinction.

Remember how your parents told you to never discuss religion or politics in public? Well, we're going to. Here we go.

I have a lovely, kindhearted, beautiful client, who when initially married, was a devout Lutheran. She married young, had two beautiful daughters, and was happy. But over time, her faith and beliefs changed, and with that, her relationship with her husband changed too. He could not understand what happened to the girl he once knew. It seemed their marriage had somehow devolved to roommate status. This is why religion is a hotbed of controversy. Faith, over time, can change, as it did for my client. Starting out, you will discover where you both stand on the religion scale. You may be more spiritual while your potential partner may be an every Sunday kind of guy or gal, or vice versa. Whatever the case, it's not only important to understand where each one is currently, but where each one may be going. Even those who are absolute in their dogma today may change their ways in a decade. Remember this and, to avoid issues in the future regarding religion, be open to the ebb and flow that we all have with our belief system. Remember, it wasn't religion that you were initially drawn to, it was the person.

Oh, those nasty politicians. And the nasty debates political ideas can spawn. Much like religion, politics can be an ever-changing perspective. Over the course of one life, we may go from neutral observer to radical lobbyist trying to preach our viewpoints. I can't tell you how many couples I talk to that have out-and-out arguments over politics. The solution: Much like religion, it's best to understand that not only may your position change, but your partner's thoughts may change as well. But, it wasn't their politics that attracted you. It was their being and their heart. Hold on to that. Although their government policy perspective may have changed, they haven't.

All grown adults have baggage. Emotional baggage that carries into each and every relationship we have, romantic and otherwise. What we have to remember with each other is that both parties, no matter how normal we seem, carry it around. Whether it's from a past lover or a bully in elementary school, those unseen wounds are there. And anything can trigger them. So, we need to honor those kooky little pieces of one another. If we are truly committed to one another, it's our job and opportunity to help heal those issues with our partner. Now, all the work isn't 100 percent yours. It is something that needs to be done together as a team. And that may sound a little daunting. But know, in the long run, healing those chinks in the armor only serve to improve and grow the relationship. So you do have a vested interest in working on it!

Drilling down a bit on the idea of baggage, let's take a look at the many folks out there in an imaginary town I have named Singleville who have one common denominator: trust issues. Trust, although not necessarily thought of in this way, is an emotion like any other. And let's be real. Emotions are typically based in sound reason and logic. In that vein, trust issues can come from something very tangible or can seemingly be created from nothing in one's own mind. Unfortunately, regardless of the genesis, those pesky trust issues are hard to get through. Not to mention that they are often transferred to an individual who had nothing to do with the origination. If you are the one with the trust issues here's my advice: stop. You and you alone have control over the way you feel. It is not anyone's job to prove themselves to you. You have to be ready to move through your issue. Own it and release it. Remember, we don't act upon every impulse. Nor do we need to act upon every emotion. Understandably, no one wants to be hurt. However, if trust doesn't exist in a relationship, it stays one-dimensional and never progress naturally.

You would think that love and respect would go hand-in-hand. Surprisingly, they do not. As we all know, we can detest another human being but still respect them. The same goes for love. We can love another but have little respect for their character. (Just talk to anyone that has had experience in an abusive relationship. Love exists, but lack of respect is 100 percent the case.) But, as much as they don't have to go hand-in-hand, in any long-term relationship, you need to have mutual respect for each other. Respect encompasses not only thoughts but dreams, aspirations, goals, and ideals. Respect tells your companion that although I may not agree with you at all times, I'll listen, honor (that's a biggie), process, and engage in the foundation that is you. The only way that we can grow in a relationship is to respect one another.

Admittedly, I'm horrible at this next point, but it's extremely valid nonetheless. Fight right. Man, those tempers of ours sure do make things more difficult sometimes. And although we love and cherish each other, that love goes right out the window when we are angry, hurt, or upset. I don't believe that there is one person out there who hasn't said something in haste to their partner that they have not deeply regretted. The best thing we can do is to learn from that lesson or situation. We must try to become better at expressing what the hurt is rather than lashing out at the one that we love the most in the world. Making I statements (I feel _____, or I am sad because _____,) is the best way to go about understanding where each other is wounded. From there, you can move on to discussing the miscommunication, misunderstanding, or whatever prompted the issue in the first place. And remember this: name-calling is never, ever okay or an effective tool in fighting fair.

Ultimately, love is the basis for everything else that comes with a relationship. And love isn't the romance and good times. Love is the tough stuff... the challenges and the conflict that comes with every relationship. Remember, love isn't about loving the best in a person. It's knowing the worst and loving them in spite of it.

Nineteen

If You Think They Are Cheating

How's that for a harsh chapter title? Not to mention a tough reality. But it really is the truth. Let me explain …

First off, look at the situation as rationally as you can. Don't assume the worst. Analyze your own insecurities and be open and honest with your partner. You need to be vulnerable and open up if you feel that your partner is not fully there or committed to the relationship.

This isn't about being the jealous kind. If you have had issues with jealousy and trust throughout every relationship that you've been in, then the issue is with you. Perhaps that inherent trust issue comes from something within. Maybe you don't feel worthy of being in a great relationship. Maybe you thrive on the drama of a potential conflict. Whatever the case, if that behavior sounds like something that permeates every relationship for you, move on. This part of the book is not for you. Get yourself to some therapy and work that out in there.

I'm talking to those guys and gals that really, in their heart of hearts, believe that their partner is cheating on them. Something is eating away, unseen, giving them cause for concern. There's a reason that suspicion exists. And there is good, sound logic in following up on it, and that, dear reader, is the whole point. Follow up. You can't let this feeling sit around and fester like an open wound. You need to get answers and give some finality to what you, in your heart, are feeling.

First things first: Why are you suspicious? Did you find a piece of paper with an unknown number on it? Are you getting odd calls where they hang up if you answer? Is your guy or girl just being really sketchy about where they were, or where they are going? Obviously, the first course of action is to simply ask them. It might be painful. The response may cause a conflict. But, as I tell all of my clients, you will at least have an answer. (Note: Answers do not always mean truth.) That is where you need to start. Keep in mind that you may get a very straightforward answer that you were not hoping for. All of this is part of the process.

Something else to ponder...What do YOU consider cheating? Believe it or not, a wide breadth of experiences falls into the cheat category. What does it mean to you?

Some folks think that flirting is cheating. Personally, I flirt with anyone, regardless of gender, so that certainly doesn't cause heartache in my book. But, for some, it really does. For others, it's having any sort of romantic feelings. For example, a simple crush or even feeling a deeper connection, other than friendship, to someone besides your partner, can constitute cheating. Of course, most of us would agree that physical touch in any capacity is infidelity. Holding hands, kissing, and sex, for most, meet the criteria.

Another suggestion is to talk to your family. Let's face it. We typically aren't terribly objective to our partner when involved in a relationship. Our family sees things we may not. Not to mention that they, hopefully, have our best interest at heart. However, along with the love that our family has for us, they don't want to hurt us, either. So, they may hold back on things that they perceive or know. Ask them their thoughts. Ask them if they've heard anything suspicious. Here again, we may get answers that we would rather not hear. Be prepared. And whatever happens, regardless of the status of infidelity, don't hold the feedback against them. Take in the information, utilize it as necessary, and move on.

If you are just dating (and by dating I mean in any relationship other than an exclusive, romantic relationship), you need to let your suspicions pass. If you haven't had the commitment discussion and both agreed to be monogamous, then you don't have the right to be suspicious. Although you may be a very committed person and not a serial dater, that doesn't mean that whomever you're dating has the same conviction. If you haven't made the specific decision to be exclusive, then you can't take umbrage at their behavior.

It's up to you to be the investigator. If you've asked the question, gotten an answer, and still feel as if something is awry, then you need to dig deeper. I always find it fascinating when people ask, get a response, still feel skeptical, yet never dig deeper. It's almost as if they'd rather be uncomfortable than find out the truth. But I digress. There are various methods of doing some pretty passive research. Ask the same question in different ways. See if the answer changes. Look around their car. Have things been moved or added that would be unusual for them? Take note: Please make sure to not break any privacy rules unless you have concrete evidence that you feel you need to explore. If you feel it's necessary, go the extra mile and hire a professional private investigator.

We've all heard the saying that love is blind. Then add deaf and mute. That doesn't mean that you have to be stupid in addition. If you're feeling compelled to investigate, don't make yourself out to be the bad guy. We act upon other hunches. Work through this one as well. The greatest result is that you can prove yourself wrong, put your suspicions aside, and move on to a better relationship. Too frequently we find ourselves pooh-poohing our thoughts and notions, telling ourselves we're being overly sensitive or jaded. That may be the case, but if it is, by doing a little soul searching we can determine that readily.

We need to listen to our gut. It guides us, protects us, and warns us of upcoming issues. It tells us to proceed with caution not only in relationships but in all aspects of life. Very rarely, if you really think about it, do gut reactions steer us wrong. It's when we dismiss that feeling and go against ourselves where we typically misstep and find ourselves in regret.

So, let's just say you find out that you were right. Your partner is cheating. You've discovered evidence beyond a shadow of a doubt. What do you do? That's up to you, but something you may want to consider during the process. Do you part ways? Can you find it in your heart to forgive? (I don't believe in the "forget" part.) However you choose to move forward, just make sure it is really moving on. You cannot change what happened. The past is the past and whatever your choice is, make the unconditional vow to grow in this experience.

If you find that your perceptions were validated and the cheating occurred, you need to make one big, gigantic decision, and that is, to trust again. Although it's going to be up to you whether you trust this individual going forward, you have to recommit to the idea that not all folks you will encounter will behave the same way. You may need to heal. That takes time. However, know within your heart that although this relationship didn't pan out the way you'd hoped, the future is bright. You can make the best out of what is to come no matter what you choose to do!

Here is a perfect example of a woman acting on her hunch to discover that her boyfriend was cheating on her. A teary-eyed gal in her late twenties came to my office several years ago for a face-to-face appointment and was quite upset about her so-called relationship. When we sat down, she explained what had happened a couple weeks earlier.

She found out that her current, live-in boyfriend was cheating, plain and simple. Although he wouldn't admit it to her, she had very sound evidence of what had been transpiring over the last several months with another gal. Being the little investigator, she found out their patterns, where the other woman's home was, and, most importantly, when their next meeting would be.

When the day the boyfriend and other woman planned to rendezvous rolled around, my client went over to the woman's house to confront both the boyfriend and the mistress. As she approached the home, the boyfriend saw her through a window. He knew exactly what was to come. He was in for a verbal assault. As such, he high-tailed it up into the attic, although only clothed in a towel as he had just exited the shower. He was a simple coward and ran away hoping to avoid her wrath, the truth.

Upon approaching the house, my client immediately saw that her boyfriend's car was brazenly parked out front—confirming her worst suspicions and fears. He was there. Appropriately, she parked her car and furiously walked to the front door and knocked. The woman answered, and my client plowed her way into the home intent on confronting the other woman and the boyfriend at the same time. However, it was only the lady of the house that she initially saw.

My client initiated the confrontation by stating that she knew what was going on and that she knew that the boyfriend was there. Although the mistress admitted to the affair with the boyfriend, she denied that the mutual boyfriend was actually at the house, saying he had left a while back. As my client continued to make accusations, the other woman tired of the battle and eventually turned her back and tried to walk away from my client, proceeding upstairs to the home's second-floor bedrooms. The mistress was hoping that my client would just leave her home and not follow her upstairs. But that was not the case, since my client was a woman scorned and intent on getting a pound of flesh from everyone involved.

She (the client) followed the other woman right upstairs, continuing to profess her disgust and anger at the entire situation, letting her know about both past events and the future plans that she and the boyfriend had made that obviously didn't include her (the mistress). My client followed the other woman into a bedroom on the second floor hoping to hear that, never again, would the mistress see the boyfriend. But that rant was cut short.

As the two women were standing face to face in the bedroom, they heard a loud creak and then a major break.

Then all hell broke loose. The boyfriend, who had been in the attic this entire time, fell through the bedroom ceiling, still wrapped in the towel from the shower. Needless to say, at a minimum, my client's suspicions that he was still in the home were confirmed.

Now back to my client and me sitting in my office …

So, upon telling me this quite interesting story, she asks me this one, singular question: Should I get back together with him and give him another chance? There it is folks. Sometimes you just don't need a psychic. Of course, my answer was an abrupt "Hell no!" Most likely followed by "are you kidding me?" and an offer to kick this guy's butt.

I picked up that this man was a perpetual cheater who continually sabotaged one relationship after another, and that she should run far, far away. He had no intention of marrying her, which was her ultimate objective. Love is blind, so they say, and I made it clear to my client she had lost all sight of what was happening in her relationship.

I am human, after all, and girls need to stick together sometimes. But she needed someone who was objective who didn't know her or her so-called boyfriend or her family that could see the entire story and tell her to just say no and dump his sorry ass. Objectivity is vital when assessing whether or not to take yourself out of the equation. What would you do if you were not in the situation? Sometimes you need to listen to your own advice.

Another thing: If you find there was an indiscretion, don't blame the third person. Although it takes two to tango, you, personally, are only in the romantic relationship with the one person. It is quite easy to blame the other party involved, as they typically are not a part of your conversations working through the conflict. It's not to say that the third party isn't a part of the issue, but do not allow the one you love to deflect the responsibility to someone else not in the room. What happened was and is between you and your partner. Although a third party is involved, they are not privy to the inner workings of your relationship. Keep the blame where it needs to be—with the one who chose to step out of the bounds of commitment.

Lastly, in a relationship where there was a cheat, one of the worst things you can do is ask yourself "Why?" Let me clue you in on something I've discovered over two decades worth of readings for others who've been in the same predicament. There isn't any right answer. Unfortunately there aren't words to make everything okay or perfectly understood. There may be thousands of excuses. There may be hundreds of reasons. But I have never come across one that has made everything right. The only thing you can do to start healing is to follow your heart and work on yourself to move forward. However, that needs to happen for you.

In a perfect world, you are going to find out that your suspicions were incorrect. You may have come across a misunderstanding to pique your interest. Maybe you overheard something incorrectly. Rejoice in the fact that you were proven wrong. Here again, this is the time to move on. Don't sit around letting the suspicion rent space in your head. Let it go. Become a more trusting and loving person in your relationship!

Twenty

Abusive Relationships

I literally got a knot in my stomach just starting this section of the book. It's not easy to talk about something so heinous. But it needs to be said, and understood. Far too many good folks I talk to each and every day are either in an abusive relationship or have been in an abusive situation. If you have not directly or indirectly been in an abusive relationship, thank goodness. Believe it or not, that is not the norm. This piece of material may not be fun, exciting, or filled with humor. Be forewarned. However, it's something that goes on behind closed doors each and every day in every community. Although I'm no therapist, I do speak with those men and women who have encountered abuse. And I'll be damned not to be a voice for them here in this book.

Maybe the best way to start this part of the book is with my own personal experiences. So many times we get into abusive relationships due to our experiences growing up as children. I know I had my fill. My DNA dad (the Dad I refer to otherwise throughout this book is my stepdad, the man who really raised me) had a temper. I could regale you with countless memories and stories of anger-fueled moments, but I'll just share this one with you. My DNA dad, mom, and I were making the trek home from my grandparents' farm in southern Minnesota. Although my DNA dad was driving, he apparently became unfamiliar with how to get home. I assumed he was taking a new route. When my mom simply suggested taking a left, he thought the appropriate response was to punch her in the face, with little me in the back seat as a witness. I was about four years old, and that moment is burned into my memory. Sadly, my mom had a black eye for days, but I think that was the least of her injuries. I remember seeing her take out that yellow stick of cover-up day after day to try to hide what he did. Although he did it, she took on the shame as hers alone. She didn't want to go out. She didn't want to share what happened. She just took it all on herself and internalized the fear, disrespect, and embarrassment. Shortly thereafter, scared for what else he could do, not only her, but to her daughter (me), she filed for divorce after eleven years of marriage. Fortunately, this was the last time he would physically abuse her. But there were others. I won't share them with you now, as further points need to be made.

So my mom got out of an abusive marriage and met and married the man who is now my dad. Although I lived a pretty typical childhood, the abusive pattern I had witnessed carried over into my dating. Just after high school, I began a long-term relationship with a local boy. All in all, we dated for about two tumultuous years. He was part of a big family, and every member of that family loved to party. Unfortunately alcohol and drug abuse reared its head with more than one of the siblings. And I was lucky enough to attach myself to one of the worst abusers. This boy was the baby of the family. And when you're one of seven, when it gets around to parenting, mom and dad are just tired. So they let things go that might not have flown earlier with the older kids.

My boyfriend, Matt, was willing to try any type of illegal substance. And honestly, as we were years before the legal drinking age, pretty much everything was illegal. But, having six older siblings, a couple of whom had their own addictions, makes it pretty easy to procure whatever your heart desires. And Matt took full advantage. Beer and pot were easy to get his hands on. But the spectrum of what he would try and ultimately use was endless. Cocaine, methamphetamine, you name it. And there I was, standing by his side, just trying to keep him upright and prevent an overdose. I'll tell you what: once you see that side of drugs, you'll want nothing to do with them.

As I mentioned, Matt and I dated quite a while. At one point, I actually called a meeting with his mom and dad to share my observations and my fears about his drug addictions. I fully expected that he would break up with me as soon as he found out. But, like many addicts, he understood that he had a problem and apologized to me for it, promising me that he would straighten up and try. And what can I say? I was young. I thought he would make better choices going forward. He didn't.

One afternoon, the entire family was getting together at the parents' house for a sibling reunion. The married siblings were bringing their spouses and kids. Those who were dating were bringing their significant others. So I was included. Matt started pounding the beers. Getting more and more slurry and sloppy, he decided to go lay down in his room. After a couple hours, his darling little nephew and his family made it to the get-together. The boy wanted to go see his uncle. I thought enough time had passed that Matt may have sobered up enough to reconnect with the party. The little nephew and I went up to his room, knocked on the door, and Matt told us to come in. Unfortunately, the time away hadn't helped. When we entered, his nephew rushed up to the bed wanting to play. Matt shoved him, cursed at him, and said some pretty terrible things. At this point, the nephew started to cry. He didn't understand what was going on. He was only four years old. I escorted him back downstairs, incensed. Then I stormed back upstairs to have it out with Matt, my mistake. I was sick at what happened. "Whatever your issue is, you don't hurt a child in my presence," I loudly explained to Matt. Matt's solution: Shove me into a wall. Then grab my wrist to such a point it later swelled up around my watchband—to the point that you couldn't see the watch. As he was manhandling me, he decided to pull a gun out of a holster he had hanging around his bedpost.

As I stood up, trying to regain balance, he pulled the gun, loaded it with bullets, and told me he was going to shoot me. My response was calm but quick, so with pride I told him if you shoot me for protecting a young child, it will be worth taking the bullet. At that point, he seemed to lose some steam, and I was able to make it out of the room. Leaving the room, I found his mother sitting there on the stairs, listening to the entire event. She was too afraid to enter the room to try and stop the attack. And I'll leave it at that. So, when I speak to abuse, I know what I'm talking about.

My entire point sharing this with you, dear reader, is that abuse, whether physical or psychological, often becomes ingrained at a very young age. Growing up with any sort of abuse often leads to encounters with it in our adult lives, no matter how aware of the situation we are. We adjust to it. It's not so much that we can't recognize it and know that it is wrong, but more so that we relate to it. It's familiar. And, because we are often in love with those who abuse, we think that maybe this time we can love just enough to make the bad behavior stop. Unfortunately, our love can never stop an abusive situation. The only love that will stop an abuser is love for oneself. The anger and hostility that they have and project onto others is really deep down personal hate and resentment for themselves.

I think that we all understand what physical abuse is. It's any sort of unwanted physical touch. Hitting, shoving, sexual assault (including everything from forced, nonconsensual sex to explicit talk), even poking can be seen as a physical attack. Then there is the psychological abuse. I use this term to encompass what some call mental and emotional abuse. Frankly, I don't see how you can have one without the other. You screw with someone's mind and, ultimately, it's going to affect their emotional state. Psychological abuse can include name-calling, yelling, intimidation, put-downs, negative judgmental statements—the type of abuse that creates the unseen bruises and black eyes. It wounds the soul. Although I believe that psychological abuse can and does exist without physical abuse, I do not believe that physical abuse cannot exist without psychological abuse.

Any form of intimidation is viewed as abuse. Threats of any sort are absolutely seen as a technique used by abusers. We all know that when we were children we heard, "Just wait until your father gets home!" From there, what we conjured up in our mind was, likely, much worse than the actual punishment itself. Same principle applies here. Verbal threats of physical intimidation are scary. Whether or not the threat becomes real or not is irrelevant. Implying any sort of abusive behavior is just as bad as the actual deed itself.

Now, bear in mind, disagreements and outright arguments aren't abuse. Of course, there may be upset moments or hurt emotions, but conflict occurs each and every day. No matter how deep, caring, and love-filled your relationship, it's natural, normal, and healthy to have a fight now and again. It is how you fight that becomes the issue. As I stated before, no matter how mad or angry you or your partner becomes, there is never a need for abuse.

A few tips on how to fight fair: First, make the issue the only issue. There isn't a need to take steps back and bring up other past conflicts. Stay on topic. Second, always remember that although you are at odds over the issue, you still respect and love your partner. No need to belittle them. Using "I statements," such as, "I feel ________," is a great way to keep the conversation on the up and up. Another tip: If your partner gives you credit, appreciate and acknowledge that understanding. Don't look for more. Acknowledging positive steps during a conflict can really work to resolve the issue much more quickly. If things become too heated, take a minute to walk away. Leave the room. Leave the building if you have to. Taking a pause gives you both some time to clear your minds. Lastly, forgive. And mean it. If you come to a point where you are seeing that you may have misunderstood something, own it. Ask for forgiveness. Alternatively, if your partner wants to apologize, go there.

You have nothing to gain by keeping the hostility going. Forgive and then really, really let it go and move on.

Unfortunately, I talk to both men and women in abusive relationships who stay together for the kids. Although the sentiment is understood and well meant, the outcome is pretty grim. Staying in an abusive relationship creates a few problems. First of all, you are teaching your children that abuse is okay in a relationship. If you are going to tolerate it, then they should expect and tolerate the same behaviors in their adult relationships. Another issue: You are showing your children that you don't respect yourself. No one with self-respect should put up with any sort of abusive behavior. And if you won't (or choose not to) respect yourself, how are the kids supposed to respect you and listen to your guidance? By staying, you are creating a conflicting atmosphere in which you ask them to mind what you say, but show that your are not willing to take control of your own life.

Another issue is that the parenting suffers. All abusive relationships put a wedge between the abusee and the abuser. Parenting is about teamwork. And I don't care how great of an actress/actor you are, your kids will see the divide. Any pain your children may feel because you left the situation will be multiplied by staying.

Unfortunately, another reason why good people stay in critical, abusive relationships is the alleged embarrassment they feel about being in the situation. Nothing could be further from the truth, but, unfortunately, the abuser often creates a psychological headspace where the abusee feels they will be shunned by those who love them. Being in an abusive relationship isn't small potatoes. It's major. If you are in a situation that has any abuse, find a support system and quickly; you will see that there are not only those who love and understand, but can relate. A shocking statistic from the FBI reports that four women a day are beaten to death by a husband, boyfriend, or cohabitating partner in abusive relationships. These are wonderful people who just didn't feel they could find a way out. Don't become a statistic. If you don't feel you can confide in anyone you know personally, there are great organizations to contact such as the National Domestic Violence Hotline at 1-(800)-799-SAFE (7233). Domestic violence is still the single biggest threat of injury to women—more than heart attacks, cancer, strokes, car accidents, street violence, and rapes combined.

Unfortunately the statistics for men being abused aren't as prominent. But make no mistake; men are victims of abuse as well. As we, culturally and economically, are shifting as a society, we are finding the trend toward abuse to males becoming more and more staggering. However, because too many men feel emasculated by the abuse, they aren't coming forward as readily. But, more and more cases are being documented and information is coming forward. This isn't a gender-specific issue.

If you are in an abusive relationship, remember life is a series of choices, and you do not have to accept the spot you are in. No one deserves to be in any sort of abusive situation. Although the choices may be hard, there are always choices. There are resources out there to help you—you are not alone. There are friends, family, co-workers, and professionals who want nothing more than what is best for you. They love and care about you. Reach out to them today. Do not feel shame in asking for help. You did not create this awful situation you are currently stuck in. Many more people than you know have gone through abusive relationships, and they can relate and they can assist. Anyone worth having in your life will not judge you; they want and desire to help. Reach out to them now and put yourself on a new, safe, and happy path. Get out now; you won't regret it. Rather than being a victim, look to change your personal story. Imagine being able to use your story of survival to help out someone else. Imagine the inspiration you could provide someone who is in the same boat. Helping yourself will in turn help others. But you need to save yourself before you can become the savior of others.

Part Three

Take Stock, Learn, Move On, and Try Again

Twenty-One

Blame Is for Suckers

I believe it's a Japanese philosophy that emphasizes the idea that blame is a waste of time. I couldn't agree more. Although I think people need to be held accountable for the situations they create, searching for the person to blame rarely solves anything. Of course, this rule isn't for criminal activity. In that case, I wholly endorse finding the culprit. However, in romantic relationships, I see far too many couples taking up far too much time trying to place blame on each other.

I think we could all agree that we've all made a mistake or two. We're human after all. And, hopefully, in those situations that we have hosed up, I trust that we take responsibility for said hose up. We are adults who understand that no one is perfect. But that nasty blame card can come into play. Let me ask you this: If you were to be blamed for something, regardless of the issue or your guilt or innocence, is your first instinct to defend, deny, and possibly excuse your behavior (if conceding to any point of contention)? My point is that it's human nature to push back on blame, even if you are 100 percent responsible. Blame puts people on the defensive. No getting around it. And putting anyone on defense doesn't create a great atmosphere for communication. And what does poor communication lead to? Poor relationships, that's what. Blame is a sure-fire way to Argumentville, which is just west of Singleville and south of Fight Town. Unless you're looking for a conflict, don't blame.

Blame assigns the catalyst for the hurt/pain—it doesn't really fix anything. You may feel justified in getting your partner to submit to some sort of fault, but what exactly does it accomplish? It just justifies your victimization. And let me tell you this, honey, victim doesn't look pretty on anyone. Essentially blame is an arm wrestling match. You don't win any awards, there isn't any applause, and it really doesn't hold any ground for future use. Just like those silly guys in a bar, after a few beers, needing to find some feat of strength to make them feel superior, so works blame.

Let me tell you another truth about blame. Blame simply creates more blame. How you ask? Think about it, in defense mode, the first thing you reach for is a way to justify your actions. How do we do that? With a good old, "Well you did _____, so don't be mad at me!" Very adult, but we all do it. From there, as we draw on the anger of the moment, we go churning up any and all transgressions our mind can conjure to defend ourselves, often by redirecting the conversation to our partner's misdeeds. This cycle of blame is just silliness on top of more silliness.

Not to mention that blame can take an awful lot of time. Any sort of argument isn't a great use of time. I think we can all agree on that. And, once the blame train leaves town, even if you get your partner to concede, you are still, most likely, left with the original conflict. After getting all worked up on the blame piece, you'll want to hash out the feelings, hurt, and actions. But what about the solution? Isn't that what everyone really wants? We want to be understood and forgiven. We also want to come to an agreement that includes a plan for what to do if the situation arises again. It's just that simple. Blame, in any form, really has no place in healing. It only creates more hurt. That I promise.

Lastly, before rushing to blame, or even approaching a conflict, take a minute to walk in the offender's shoes. Is the offense really heinous? Was it done with malicious intent? Probably not. Most likely, your loved one just didn't think, or didn't know. Who are we to think we are without sin? We have all said something ghastly without meaning it. We have all overstepped a boundary where we didn't know there was one. As such, keep in mind your own faults and flaws before exhausting time and effort in finding fault not only in your partner, but in all relationships. It's been said that no one ever regretted being silent in an argument.

The bottom line here isn't when to engage in a fight. They're going to happen. That's part of relationships and being in love. We not only hurt those we love most, but they hurt us the most deeply. It's part of the deal. However, take the time to act, react, and argue the way that you should—like a grown-up. Children, because they don't know any better or have the right words to express their full emotions, place blame. You are older and hopefully a bit wiser than that. Tap into that wisdom and don't play the blame game.

Twenty-Two

Letting Go

It happens. Although we try to make it work, through one condition or another, it's not going to. So we need to let go of the relationship. Maybe you have changed. Maybe your partner made a poor decision that you cannot agree with or forgive. Whatever the case, when talking about relationships, you need to, in fact, I'd say you MUST talk about the breakup.

For the breakee (the one who's being dumped): Yeah. You are going to feel rejection. It is totally normal and reasonable to have a bit of a pity party. We all have to wallow in the sadness for a bit. And that's the key word: *bit*. This isn't a forever state. The world goes on. Pull yourself up by your bootstraps and get back out there. Just because this relationship didn't work out doesn't mean another, totally viable, exciting relationship isn't around the corner. This is the best time in the world to join a gym, get a makeover and revamp yourself, and get on to bigger and better!

For the breaker (the one initiating the breakup): You've probably been mulling this over for days, maybe even weeks or months. Keep that in mind. You've had time to prepare. Be kind. (We'll talk more about that later.) And by all means, don't get smug. Let your soon-to-be ex-partner know that you're hurting too. Silly as it may seem, to know that the other party in the relationship is hurting tends to ease individual pain. Another pointer: Make it quick. No breakup ritual needs to be dragged out to come to some point of understanding and mutual conclusion. Say what you have to say and then part ways. And I mean part ways literally. If at all possible, woman up/man up and do it in person, face-to-face like an adult. One other thing is to not be the schmuck that breaks up via text.

Which kind of leads to something that's relatively new, at least to the over-thirty crowd, and that is the social media aspect of the breakup. In the matter of moments, friends, family, co-workers, and acquaintances can know our relationship status. Although I'm extremely fond of social media, I've seen it used in relationships in horrible, vindictive ways. The public outburst and humiliating comments that are posted on some people's public pages can be scathing. Remember this: no one, ever, ever was faulted for taking the high road or for keeping personal details personal. I get it. When we go through a breakup, many of us want to share the details. And that's okay. In fact, it's healthy to discuss what transpired with those you are close to privately. Keeping it private is the key. However, it's simply not necessary to have (for example) Sally, who sits in the office cube kitty-corner from you, know the dirty details.

Sure, spilling it all is cathartic, and some of your acquaintances may even join you in the bashing of the ex, but consider this—you may end up getting back together. You never know. I've seen the most heinous breakups in which the couple later reconciled and rekindled the romance. And then what? You'll have a lot of explaining to do.

Breakup Tips

Let me make some suggestions to those who are thinking of breaking it off with their current partner (and these stem from countless regrets I've heard in personal readings throughout the years):

Tip #1: No Breakup Sex

I cannot tell you how many scorned individuals were hurting, looking for affection, and gave in to that temptation, only to feel remorseful and disgusted afterward. Interestingly enough, when we, as humans, experience a loss, there is a chemical that is released into our bodies that causes us to crave physical affection. Hence, the desire to have one more physical connection with the ex. However, just because biology is at work here doesn't mean that we have to follow through. Heck, we often feel hungry and crave different foods, but move past those. This is the same thing. Don't do it. You'll live to regret it.

Tip #2: Don't Be Mean

Just don't be mean. There's no reason for it. And, frankly, there isn't a cause to be rude either. If you're adult enough to have a relationship with someone, be an adult and act like it in the breakup. If nothing else, remember and respect what you two once had, even if it's long gone. Here, again, it's about taking the high ground. Can you be honest? Of course. Can you share examples? Absolutely. Your former mate could even find this to be informative and constructive advice for the future. But it's not about dredging up the past and rehashing it. You have made your decision. Follow it through with dignity, kindness, and respect.

Tip #3: Do It in Public

No, not that! But if it's at all possible, meet at a public place. And notice that I said *meet*. If you both transport yourselves to one location, other than one another's home, you don't have to deal with that extremely awkward drive home together. You can both quietly leave and lick your wounds respectively. Additionally, this pretty much squelches any chance of breakup sex. Also note that I said *public place*, which decreases the chance of shouting and hysterics, as most of us would rather not make a scene. It creates more of a subdued, calm transition. Although you may be faulted for breaking it off in public, explain that you wanted a neutral atmosphere where both of you could feel comfortable.

It's Done—Now What?

No matter how it happens, it hurts. And we dwell on the exact words more than under any circumstances, even if they're cliched. This is okay. We've all heard it,whether it came from one of our favorite sitcoms or happened in real life: The "It's not you, it's me" excuse. And there's validity to it. So, if you are on the receiving end of it, embrace it. People change. It's a fact of life and something that we all go through. Hopefully, as we make those changes, our relationships grow and deepen, allowing those changes to be incorporated. However, sometimes they don't. And the new perspective is counteractive to the relationship. If that's really, truly the case, then you have every right to utilize that reasoning. However, be prepared to expand upon and explain where those changes have taken place, internally and externally. It's only fair, if you're going to express yourself that way, that you have examples. Again, use the breakup as an opportunity for growth on both your parts.

So the breakup happened. And you're the breakee. You didn't see this coming. And here you sit, sad and blue. A suggestion for you is do not wait around. Clinging to a glimmer of hope that something may change and help reignite your relationship doesn't mean that you sit around pining for your loved one in hopes they see the light. In fact, work the opposite side of things. Make yourself more available and attractive to all parties (new and old). Take up a new hobby. Get a gym membership. Learn a new skill. Whatever it is, you take control of your life and what is to come. Doing nothing will never create the change that you want in your life. The moment you get moving is the moment that the Universe brings you new opportunities!

Now let's talk about the good old rebound. Yep, rebound relationships happen, and they happen all the time. I'll go out on a limb and even say they're healthy—as long as you understand, acknowledge, and embrace the fact that they are temporary. A rebound is meant to be fun and spontaneous, a reminder of the joy of the joy of dating and relationships. They're not meant to be the next big thing. Rebounds are meant to bring you back to balance from the hiccup that was a breakup. So enjoy them but really understand what they're about. It's about finding that self-confidence, self-esteem, and inner glow that new relationships bring. A rebound fling can be helpful for you to get over the hurt and it may launch you back into the dating pool.

Staying in Touch

Unless the breakup was particularly unsavory or resulted in someone moving out of the state, you'll probably see your ex once in a while through common co-workers, a shared circle of friends, and maybe even while diving back into the dating pool. It's best if you are prepared for this. Having contact with someone even as an acquaintance can stir up emotions, and even after starting a few hobbies and having a good rebound, this question almost always seems to come up.

What if you two do get back together?

Before even approaching the idea of getting back together, ask yourself these super-important questions: Is the reason that you broke up still there in any form? Is the issue still looming? Does the situation still affect you? If the answer is "yes" to any of it, stay away. You're not doing yourself or your mate any favors by giving it a go simply due to optimism. If they are in the same place and if you still have the same thoughts and feelings, you need to move on. Although loving feelings can exist long after a breakup (even an extremely rough one), that doesn't necessarily mean that love is going to bring each of you to a new or better place. It's great to have good memories. And it's even better to be able to look back at situations and see how you would do things differently. However, all that lovely hindsight doesn't mean that you should go back to what was.

So, let's say you ask yourself that question again. Does the breakup issue(s) still exist? And your answer is no. Great! Fantastic! That means that someone has grown! Certainly worth commendation! Although the growth and change happened, it doesn't mean that you should just jump right back into things. Remember to start back at the beginning. Either you or your partner changed. This is amazing. So, that means you're working with new material, and that, dear reader, needs to be explored and embraced. Jumping right back in where you were doesn't allow the time to respect and get to know this new piece of the individual. Honor it. Go back to the courting stage. Heck, it was probably the most exciting part of your relationship! Get to know each other again and let things re-evolve! In all my years, in all my readings, I have never heard anyone remark that they regretted taking their time in a relationship.

Now, after the breakup, the big question remains: Can we still be friends? I'm not going to lie. For me, personally, I just needed to be done. Call me shallow. Call me simple. Whatever it was, I just didn't feel the need to continue the relationship in any form. The reason I mention this is that I think that in today's world we feel pressure from society to be civilized and sophisticated, which means keeping our exes around us. If you can do that, great! You're a bigger person than I. However, if it continues/maintains the hurt, why would you do that to yourself? You don't have an obligation to be friends with anyone. Although I appreciate that we all want to be liked and have lasting friendships, we don't have to force-feed them if they are painful. Remember that. And if you are a person who is really good with having an ex as a friend, but the ex balks at the idea, honor that as well. That's how they feel, and it should be respected.

One last suggestion—one that may sound a little silly. Hollywood has it right. When celebrity couples break it off, the press releases go out. Cheesy as they may be, the verbiage in them is pretty awesome. They speak to honoring the relationship that they once had, respecting the privacy, healing the hurt, and so forth. There will come a time where you'll have to announce, either to an individual or to a group, that you've parted ways from your former love. Keep those corny press releases in mind. By saying those sorts of things, you're not only respecting your former partner, but you're also respecting what you formerly had. Not to mention, you look like a champ for taking the high road.

Twenty-Three

After the Breakup

I can't tell you how many tales of woe I hear from sweet, kindhearted people after they have had a breakup. Whether they're big or small, those partings will take the wind out of anyone's sails. It's hard. But what I get asked about most is if how they are feeling or handling things is right. My answer: of course. What is right for you is right for you. But I get the question. Everyone wants to know if what they are going through is typical.

Again, there are no absolute, steadfast rules to healing. Nor is there anything to hasten the healing or quiet the hurt. I know, I'm being a downer again, but it's the truth. When I get asked, "How do I make the hurt go away?" my heart hurts right along with my client's. But, sad to say, I don't own a magic fairy wand to fix any circumstance, let alone have the cure for a broken heart. You have to do what you have to do to get through the pain or breakup. Outside of breaking the law, I'm open to any and all modalities of healing. Some reach for a self-help book. Other folks get their hair done. (Yes. Guys do this too. Color, plugs, etc.) Some just need to be alone and tend to their wounds. Whatever is right for you. There isn't one right or wrong way for individuals. Friends and family are going to make suggestions, try to get you out and about…all good stuff that you should give a try, if you like. But you just really dig deep and do what feels good and healing to you.

If I may, I would like to make some suggestions of what not to do after the breakup.

Drunken texting! Boy oh boy have I heard some stories. Now, whether you are the breaker (the one that initiated the breakup) or the breakee, this is a no-no. If you, being the breaker, start getting all liquored up (tequila seems to be quite a catalyst for this behavior) and drunken text your former love, you are going to create a whole lot of mess that you will have to explain at some point. Whether it is the "I still love you" text or the "You suck and I hate you" text, you have opened a can of worms that you will likely regret the next day. What you're doing is creating confusion for the ex. They don't know you've had a six-pack in the last couple hours. They thought things were done. Now you have just opened that painful door right back up. Best solution: put the phone down.

Or maybe you're the breakee and, yes, a bottle or two of wine has been shared. You get feeling nostalgic. You grab for the phone. Here again, it may be a very sweet communication of still having feelings or it may be a harsh, curse-laden diatribe of how you're better off. In either scenario, you are opening up the door where very little good can come. A general rule of thumb: If you really feel that you have something to say post-breakup, and it comes to you during a happy hour, write it down. Put it in your pocket or purse. Check it out the next day. Still seem like a great idea? Fine. Communicate your butt off. But, 90 percent of the time you'll realize that you saved yourself a world of foolishness.

Another thing to avoid (which, also, is often nudged by booze) is the idea of getting vengeance. God bless Carrie Underwood and her song "Before He Cheats," but it's just not a place you want to go. We've all heard the stories: sugar in the gas tank, scratching the car, dumping all their stuff out in the street, even stalking and creating problems for your ex at work. I could go on, but the bottom line is that you are the one hurting, and, honestly, truly hurting someone else never, ever takes your pain away. There's a great quote (which I'll paraphrase) about resentment (which is vengeance without external action): To resent someone is like poisoning yourself and hoping that the other person will drop dead. So draw up all the mighty schemes you wish. Just keep them to yourself. Or talk them over with friends and have a good laugh. But keep it at that. No need to end up in jail over some idiot.

So, time passes. You have moved through wanting to drunken text your ex. And, you don't want to take a baseball bat to their windshield anymore. Bravo. But memories remain of the physical intimacy that you shared. And it may have been pretty darn good. All fireworkey and stuff. (Yeah, I said it. Fireworkey.) You recall times, places, even maybe a few outfits that really worked for you. This does not mean you make the random booty call. For those who don't know what a booty call is, where have you been?! In all seriousness it's when you make a call/text/email for only one thing: sex. Although you may have had the most spectacular physical connection known to man, physical intimacy confuses things, especially after a breakup. And chances are it will confuse the both of you. As I've mentioned before, there are chemicals in the brain that make us feel certain ways when we connect with someone. So, if you decide to go there again, you're going to churn up feelings that really seem true and real. This can be quite unsettling, making you wonder if the departure from the relationship was the right thing. So, just don't go there. Let sleeping dogs lie. Let it go. No relationship came back into being, honorably, through a booty call.

Since we're talking about sex, just as a booty call isn't going to magically repair your old relationship, you can't screw your way to happiness either. I know. Again, I'm pretty crass. But the fact of the matter remains. Sex, although certainly pleasurable, isn't going to bring about happiness—at least not long-term, self-worthy happiness. That comes from learning and making yourself a better person. Reflect on what transpired. Take accountability for the errors you made. Respect the person that you are. Then find that happy within. No matter how pretty (and I use pretty in a non-gender way) the person you find to have sex with, they aren't going to make you all better. The healing comes from within.

And yet another segue…

Since I'm talking about that fleeting happiness, shopping your way to happy isn't going to happen either. Oh the blessed idea of retail therapy, the pretty things to make you look good on the outside. Although I'm the first person to drag your tuckus to the mall, I'll also be the first person to let you know that ringing up credit card debt isn't going to put you in a better place. In fact, a couple months down the road, it may make you feel even worse. You'll have a pile of things yet no one to care about you. Let me tell you when shopping really, really works: When you're already happy, it's an added bonus. It can be a reward for achievement, a moment of celebration. But does it bring you out of a sad, depressed state? I'm sorry to say the answer is always no.

One thing that I always suggest to my clients who are struggling with the pain of breakup: burn the pictures. I know. I know. It's very Hollywood/romantic comedy of me. But it really helps. I've seen it. It's not about vindication. It's really about the ritual of releasing that person that once held your heart. You mind is a powerful tool. Really, it's a gateway to the heart. And, through the eyes, if the mind can see the release, the heart seems to have an easier time of it. So find a nice fire pit or put those pictures in a fireplace and set 'em ablaze. Watch them turn to ash and use that moment to mourn. Then, during the ritual, as the pictures turn to dust, know that this is the first moment of the healing process.

I'm forever astounded that people, although angry and hurt, seem to find and then date the same person over and over. STOP IT. Just because you found the carbon copy of the person that wounded you doesn't mean that you can make it work—by changing—this time. If I have one and only one piece of advice to give you, please, pretty please, get out of your comfort zone (and remember—even pain can be comfortable) and date someone different. Isn't that a unique and novel idea? It seems like common sense, but I see good men and women fall into the same exact situation as the prior relationship. Quit the pattern. Find a new habit. Just stop what you've been doing. You deserve better. Honor your intelligence and change your direction.

Now let's say you really had something serious going on. You were planning on getting married. Rings were exchanged. Do you give it back? Unfortunately, I don't have a standard answer for this question. You really have to look at all things and consider what is right. If pressed to formulate an equation for what to do when, I think longevity dictates what to do. If you became engaged quickly and just as quickly decided it wasn't going to work—give back the ring. However, if you two were together for a couple years, then became engaged and were so for a good amount of time, I think the ring is yours. The other side of this argument is that you may not want the ring and simply want to get rid of it to let go of the memories. That's totally understandable, but keep in mind that your former love may not want it either, for the exact same reasons. This is why pawnshops exist. Either way, don't rush a decision. Really take time to process what you'd like to do. There's no reason for regret in the future.

Whether it takes you two days or five months to move through the breakup, know that your process is right and perfect for you. The moral of the story is to take the time to heal, but once you move on, really move forward. Even if, by chance, you end up getting back together with your ex, be a new, changed, smarter person in the relationship. Know that your strength will carry you into the future regardless of the person beside you.

Twenty-Four

Karma and Past Lives

Everyone has issues within their relationships. If you don't, you're either an alien or a robot. We don't function like a sitcom from the 1960s. We're human and complex, and in my estimation, from the day we're born we start accumulating that emotional baggage that therapists make millions trying to decipher. But did you ever think that what you are currently going through may have deeper, more soulful connections and reasons?

Let's start with the idea of karma interceding in a romantic relationship, but before we do that, we need to all get on the same page of what karma really is.

Karma is based in the traditions of India and brought forth by Hindu, Buddhist, Jain, and Sikh religions. These religions embrace the idea of reincarnation, which we'll get into shortly, but you do not need to know about past lives to understand karma. Karma isn't good or bad. In fact, it's neutral. It's about the action to balance. Although we in the Western world have made it have more of a positive or negative connotation, it's really about the unbiased stability of energies. Where there is light, there has to be dark. Where good is able to show itself, evil (bad) has to be present. It's the cause and effect of all actions. In Christianity, we think of it as the idea of "we reap what we sow," from Galatians in the New Testament.

So, thinking along those lines, that karma isn't about the good or bad, but only the balance, we need to understand how it potentially plays out. What's so nifty (or not, depending on your personal patience level) about karma is that it has its own time frame. Often, the actions of karma may take months or years to work their way through one's life. So, we, living in our immediate, instant-gratification society, don't make the connection of something happening to us now being related to something that happened a decade (or more) ago. Cheating is a great example of how karma can come back and bite you in the ass. If you cheat on a partner, it is very likely that in the future, someone will cheat on you. The karma that comes with that most often deals with and results in trust issues. Either way it sucks, but you have to deal with the repercussions of your actions.

Now, is karma to blame (remembering that it's not good or bad…or a person) for all missteps in relationships? Of course not, because we have this lovely little thing called free will. Free will allows us to make the mistakes, or, hopefully, the successes in life. Karma may present itself in a situation, but it's how we react and respond to the issue where we can have a moment of greatness and either move through a karmic act and release it or respond poorly only to live through a similar scenario a different day. For example, you can take the high road and take a step toward strengthening your relationship with your partner and talk through any struggles in the relationship, or you can cheat on your partner and continue the vicious cycle.

Although it sounds like a Universal mockery, it's really not. All things, energies, people, relationships, and issues in life are opportunities to allow our soulful side to grow and expand. Unfortunately, we, living in the human existence have a couple hurdles to overcome. One: We tend to learn more from distress and hurt than we do from positive situations. Two: That darn ego. Our ego gets us into a lot of predicaments. It tells us that we have control. It tells us that we are better than others when it comes to education, financial status, good looks, and more. And it's because of that human ego piece that we put ourselves in relationship jeopardy by putting ourselves first. Taking ego out of the equation (and this is no small feat, believe me) simply allows truth, honesty, and forward movement in relationships.

Now, how karma may play itself out comes in a variety of different ways. But nothing that is atypical. And, unfortunately, it doesn't have a telltale sign. Wouldn't it be great if there was a karma-dar like radar? Sometimes it comes in the form of a breakup where one simply walks away. No major blowout or conflict. Just goes a different direction. This often is the case when in the past one has simply ignored another in a compromising situation without addressing the issue rather than actually dealing with it.

The best way to accurately determine whether it's a karmic issue or one brought on by yourself is to really think back and feel if there is a lesson. Obviously if there is an issue around one's convictions be it religious or political or whatever, karma can be ruled out pretty quickly. However, if you need to ponder "Why did this happen?" you can almost rest assured that karma was in play.

And karma does not only come from just this life, honey.

First, I'm going to say that I believe in the idea of reincarnation and past lives. I'm not here to change your mind. Nor do I want to stomp on your own, personal convictions. I respect all faiths and philosophies. However, since the fact is that I do believe in past lives, and a great portion of the world does as well, I want to speak to those folks too. As I mentioned earlier, however, one does not have to believe in past lives to embrace the idea of karma. They are exclusive ideas.

Let's start, as we did with the karma piece, by us all getting on the same page as we explore past lives. Various cultures and religions believe in the idea of reincarnation. However, there are some variations. Some believe that a human soul has come into being by experiencing lesser life forms. For example, one may start as an amoeba, and then move up to a gnat. From there they move up the food chain, until, ultimately, becoming a human life form. Of course, if we majorly screw up this life, we can de-evolve back into a grasshopper or some other, less complex being. On the other hand, if we make great strides, we become enlightened, not needing the physical human existence for our soul's evolution.

The other theory is that a human soul is a human soul and only reincarnates as such. However, the situation one is placed in creates the evolution. Obviously someone who is born into a wealthy family of privilege and class will have a different life than someone born to a nomadic community in a Third World country. It's within these differences that the soul finds enlightenment. Both situations have their own innate issues and benefits. However, this, the human-to-human reincarnation will be the perspective I'll be speaking to from here on out.

So, that all being said and understood, we not only have karmic influences from our current life, but bring forward those karmic issues from past lives. How is that for confusing?

I believe (again, this is a personal belief) that we all have to experience all things to really become enlightened. That being said, we have to be murdered and be the murderer. We need to be persecuted and be the one persecuting. Only through this process do we develop one of the most basic human emotions: compassion. And isn't compassion, next to love, one of the main building blocks of relationships?

A long time ago, I was told that love isn't about loving the best in a person. It's knowing the worst and loving them despite it. And if that isn't the definition of compassion, I don't know what is.

As we understand that through our past lives we can develop compassion and karma, we need to grasp the concept of the soul being eternal. Our soul, from a very scientific perspective, is energy. And it's well documented and researched in the scientific community that energy never goes away, it only changes form. With that knowledge, our soul, as it is energy unto itself, has been around for all eternity. Now back to past lives...

Our past lives, along with our karma, can influence our relationships. Who hasn't had the moment, upon meeting someone, where they have felt they have known that person for a lifetime? Conversely, who can't say that they have met someone and immediately been repelled by them? It is part of the world we live in, and we all know it happens outside logic and reason.

Past life experiences influence relationships as much as anything. Although not in our current memory, the former life situations still reside somewhere, quietly within us in our soul (often referred to as cell memory). This is why we are oddly drawn to situations that may be out of our current character. Violence is a prime example of where a bad experience in a past life can be turned into something positive in this life. For example, if someone was involved in war or perhaps died in battle, they may be very passive and have a phobia toward guns and similar violence.

We have all either seen or been the individual that has been so strong in every other aspect to our lives, yet when with a particular individual we allow ourselves to be taken advantage of. Is this coincidence maybe? No, probably not. We've also either experienced firsthand or been a part of a moment, where there wasn't any prior knowledge or education, but understanding and knowledge came forth seemingly out of nowhere. Where you or the individual shakes their head and wonders, "Where the heck did that come from?" These are great examples of past life knowledge coming forward and allowing us to grow.

Sometimes, it's just the acknowledgment of having a past life with another that creates not only a deeper bond with the individual but also with Spirit. If I may share, here's an actual story.

Steve and Cindy had been clients of mine for a long time. While at a conference they requested back-to-back past-life hypnotic regressions. (I'm also a board-certified hypnotherapist.) Cindy was first. Prior to the sessions, I explained that I'll walk them into their past. However, their soul will pick the life that is pertinent to the time being, as I don't lead to a particular place and time. When there, I'll ask questions, however I don't require or ask that my client speak, out loud, the answers. The questions are only there to help the individual observe the past life and gain information. Cindy's past-life regression went well. It was pretty textbook. I brought her out of the hypnosis and we discussed what she saw and experienced. We discussed several details down to her dress, which was a velvet-textured dress. It was most likely in the mid- to late-1800s, and included a man that she was very much fixated on. I didn't get the sense that they were married in that life, but they were very much connected.

From there, I excused Cindy from the room, and brought Steve in. Please know that I was with both of them at all times and that no exchange other than "I'll see you in a hour" took place between them. I sat Steve down and started the process. Now, even though I let my clients know that it's not necessary to answer my prompting questions out loud, some still do. And that's fine. That's their nature. Steve was one of thosse guys. As I progressed him through the past life, I heard, firsthand, what he was saying. What was shocking, even to me, was that the time, date, place, clothing, and nature of the whole past-life regression mimicked what Cindy had just told me moments ago. Steve was the man in her regression that Cindy was fixated on. He was telling me the color of her dress and where he was standing in the scene. Detail upon detail corresponded to her past life that had come through. Needless to say, I could hardly wait to get the two of them together to discuss what had happened.

As I did with Cindy, I brought Steve out of the hypnosis and then we both met up with Cindy. At this point, I told them that we all needed to sit down and discuss. They still had no idea what had transpired. We went out for tea. As we sat, I simply asked Cindy to share what she had experienced and seen in her past-life regression. As she was speaking, you could see Steve well over with emotion, knowing that his beloved bride was not only his bride in this life, but a love in a past life as well. Cindy, not understanding what was going on, was a little confused. At this time, I asked Steve to share and the both of them were really beside themselves. To come to a point where love didn't have any sort of time attached to it was pretty amazing.

Hopefully this goes to show the beauty of karma (Cindy's fixation), past lives, and past loves. The influence of what we have experienced in past lives isn't all bad. Even if it hurts at times, it allows us to grow and become more substantial partners in the romantic, love-centered relationships we choose.

Twenty-Five

What the Other Side Thinks about Love

I get countless questions from my clients about how the other side views love: new love, old love, familial love, or lost love. I could go on and on. It's great to know that we can all, despite differences in race, religion, economics, and so forth, agree that it's love that permeates all things. It is part of our soul and as the soul is eternal, so is love.

As you know, I believe that we do have various lives so the soul can encounter and experience different things. I know that we can't tie our shoes right the first time, we give it a few more whirls until we get it right, so how the heck are we supposed to get an entire life experience right in one go around? As I believe that we have had many lives,

I believe that we have had many mates, and much, much love, the romantic kind and otherwise.

So, if we come from the perspective that we have had many lives and, more than likely, we have had at least some love in each life, we have had plenty of romantic relationships. Remember that. If you feel that love is lacking in the here and now, know that it hasn't always been that way and you won't forever be without. Also, though you may be in a romantic slump, take comfort that all is divinely ordered and your soul is growing in a different way.

And on that topic of many loves … Although the partner we are with currently is where our heart is, it hasn't always been nor will it forever be that way. There's a good and sound reason why our traditional marriage vows are till death do us part. When we cross over, all of our spouses and romantic partners from each and every life are on the other side waiting to be reunited with us. Because we are human, we have to wrap our heads around finite time. But when we cross over, time becomes infinite. And with that knowing, there isn't an urgency to only be with one soul. We have eternity to connect and deepen our love for everyone we care about. So, if you have lost a romantic partner, know that of course, they are waiting for you on the other side for your reunion. But, as they understand the greater perspective of time and space, they don't expect you to be by their side 100 percent of the time, forever and ever. Nor will you want to.

And speaking of losing a spouse or partner, let's talk about moving on. In thousands upon thousands of readings I've provided over decades, I can say with absolutely certainty that I have never heard a loved one from the other side tell someone here in the physical plane that it's not okay to move on. Rarely can I say that a message comes through 100 percent, but this is one of those times. They (those on the other side) desperately want you to find love again. No one, corporeal or otherwise, wants to see anyone longing for love. It's painful. And we can all relate. Each and every one of us wants love in our life. No exceptions.

There's a great line in the opening of a television show that states love is better multiplied than divided. That's exactly the way the other side looks at love. It's about continuing on and finding another love. It's what is wanted for all of us here—to be in a state of love and to provide love for another. And although we could all say that we love our family, there is something specifically magical about romantic love. The other side wants that for us. If you have lost a partner and feel that you are ready and able, look toward finding another soul to find love with. There's no guilt or shame, and in many cases, when we're ready, if we ask, that lost loved one will help us bring that new love into our lives.

Love is about honor. When we find another person to love, it doesn't lessen the love that we have had in the past. In fact, it enhances what has come before. By loving again, we're showing the Universe that we are unwilling to give up on love and understand that love can be found in many forms. Ultimately, loving again is the greatest homage to the love that has come prior.

Far too often, people ask me if an argument that preceded the passing of a loved one is remembered. Of course, more importantly, my clients want to know if the conflict is forgiven. Here again, the answer is always yes. When we cross over, although we don't become omnipotent, we gain a broader, better understanding of all things in our lives. Quarrels are, certainly, included in that broader viewpoint. Whether it was a misunderstanding, miscommunication, or bad day, it is shown to the soul to reconcile and move on toward peace. So, if a fight occurred just prior to crossing over, know, beyond all things, that you are forgiven.

Taking that one step further, upon understanding that we are forgiven, know that you ARE still loved no matter what your conflict or disagreement may have been. Although love is an emotion, it is completely driven by energy. And science tells us that energy never dies, it only changes form. Thusly, love exists and transcends physical body death. It is carried over to the other side with greater clarity and power than we can imagine.

When wanting to connect with a loved one on the other side, a common request in readings, people are surprised to hear that they do not need to pray to them. Prayers are for you and the Divine. Our loved ones do not need your prayers. They are with Spirit, in all its glory, without pain or suffering. Let your prayers be for those here on earth. Those souls on the other side don't need it. All they wish is that you are happy, loved, and taken care of in the best of ways.

I have done hundreds of readings for clients who wished to communicate with a loved one who had crossed over, and here is just one example. I had a dear elderly client whose first husband had passed away. Subsequently, she had taken up a relationship with his best friend. She had called on me and was very concerned that her deceased husband would have issues regarding her new relationship, understandably so. When we asked him how he felt about his former wife's new companion, he conveyed a clear message of happiness that she had found love again. He gave his blessing with this union and found peace that his former wife was with someone who would care for her and that it was someone he was so fond of during his physical life! We both cried tears of joy at this message from the other side. Not long after this reading, my client and her new beau got married and are living happily ever after.

Now let's get to some of the more controversial stuff…

The topic of divorce is a big one. I cannot tell you the outpouring of concern from those of us here, worrying about the perception of divorce on the other side. No one likes divorce. Not here in the physical realm nor in Spirit. It is because of this compassion that they understand divorce. Sometimes two souls have a contracted amount of time they are meant to be together, which isn't an entire lifetime. Now, this contract isn't here on earth. This is a contract made and understood, by two souls, on the other side. Contracts like this are formed so two souls can have one shared experience, but both receive a unique experience. Then they separate to gain further experiences individually. Instances of this happening may be to bring a specific soul into the world where the two combined are needed. At other times, it's karmic, where one has created an imbalance in a past life that needs to be rectified in this one. Regardless, it is understood by Spirit, and our loved ones on the other side, that it is a necessity.

Another hot topic is homosexuality, as well as bisexuality. Back home (what I like to call the other side as it's where we began and where we will return), love, in any form, is love. However it manifests and takes shape is irrelevant. All that matters is that the love is pure, true, and from the heart. Sexual organs and gender are physical. Our soul is energetic, void of form. It is only within the body that we make distinction. So, no, the other side doesn't care about the type of body that is projecting love.

On the other side the modus operandi is love and acceptance. It's not about the physicality of love, it is about the energy and sentiment. Love is the language of the other side. It is the reason the other side exists, to carry on the love, the compassion, the goodness we created here in the physical world.

Twenty-Six

My Mama Told Me

As much as we'd like to believe that our parents don't know what is best for us, sometimes they, at least, have excellent advice. They, too, have lived lives that included dating and marriage(s). Although, times, they are a-changing, they haven't changed that much. Many of the basics still remain the same. Learn from their experience. Heck, it's free, and it may just keep you away from a little heartache.

Before I get into the specifics of particular advice, I want to share a personal story with you.

When I brought my now-husband home for the very first time, I was taken aback by my dad. (Just for clarification, my dad is actually my stepdad, as he raised me most of my life.) He actually spoke to Bobby. I know this doesn't sound very major and cordial at best. But my dad isn't really the outgoing, social type. Typically speaking, when I brought someone home, I may have gotten a grunt or nod at best for my new friend. Often it was just a glance, and Dad would go back to whatever he was doing. It wasn't that he didn't care; he realized, pretty early on, that who I was bringing home was in his words "a revolving door."

When I asked him why he engaged Bobby versus any of the other people I had brought home, he said this: He actually had a brain. It was just that simple. My dad had seen what I couldn't. Of course, I was blinded by what I thought was love. My father had the good sense to see my companions for what they were. Good, bad, or indifferent. He just didn't feel it was necessary to waste time and energy getting to know anyone that he knew wouldn't (or felt shouldn't) be around very long. Don't tell, but hearing that from my dad was a huge validation to marry the hubs. My dad knew his stuff.

A nugget that my mom shared with me, and believe it or not, this does apply to relationships: no party will ever be the same twice. Remember how, when you were in high school and college, you'd party at the friend's house whose parents had left town? Well, that situation is where this little gem stems from. I had a fantastic time at a party the prior evening and the next morning told my mom about it. I had met some great people and had a blast—everyone got along, and a lovely time was had by all. We decided to hit it up for round two the next night. I mean, heck, the parents were gone for the whole week. Why not?

Here's why. If you're looking to duplicate the same person in the same scenario and get the same results, you need to think again. Romance is science; parties are not. With individuals, although they may look the same on paper, we don't get repeated results. Just because someone may have a similar job, a similar family background, and similar personal history, doesn't make them 100 percent guaranteed to work if you've previously had success with that type of person. Finding the same person (on paper, as we call it) over and over isn't going to create the same relationship repeatedly. Embrace what was, but always be willing to try something new.

Although this probably isn't news to anyone at this point, when I was nineteen, my dad shared this nugget of wisdom: 90 percent of couples break up over the almighty buck. At that time in my life, it was news to me. As much as we want to declare that money doesn't bring us happiness, lack of it can sure bring us much anguish. It's very romantic to believe that we can all live on love, but love doesn't pay the mortgage or the heating bill. And silly us, as cultured civilians we've become accustomed to those little extravagances.

Now Dad wasn't saying I should find some sugar daddy. But he was very clear about one thing: If you invest your time in someone with financial issues, you'd best be darn certain that you want to support and work through them together. And, if you choose to marry that person, those financial problems become as much yours as they are your partner's. Make certain you're willing and able to take on that burden. Know what you're getting into. And be up front about your own credit burden.

Although this next little morsel didn't come from one of my own parents, it came from a darling, former co-worker (believe it or not, I actually held a corporate job or two), who I considered very fatherly. While at a holiday party with my husband, I ran into this co-worker and his lovely wife and asked what their secret of a thirty-plus-year, extremely happy marriage was. The response: Divorce never. Murder maybe. That's dandy, right?

Obviously, the couple was completely joking. But their point was made. It was their observation that people, upon finding themselves in conflict, were too quick to jump out of the marriage. Of course, they also believed that they saw far too many young individuals rushing into marriage as well. They believed in the sacred commitment of marriage. And they also, quite vocally, believed in the necessity of courtship. They talked about how their parents had to deal with war, long-term, long-distance separation (due to war), fertility issues, and other obstacles. None of which split them up. In fact, it made them grow stronger in the good years. They were very clear that in those tough times, you can reflect on moments where times were even tougher and remember that you, as a team, got through the mess. Good stuff. Failure was not an option.

I took a quick poll on a few of my social media accounts asking those folks there if they, too, had received any great pieces of advice from their parents. A couple repeated themselves time and time again. I want to share those with you now.

First, the ladies, overwhelmingly, heard from their moms to watch a man with his mother. Here, again, what an absolute gem of insight. How a man treats his mother is very much a telltale sign as to how a man will treat a long-term commitment/wife. Now, like every rule, there are exceptions. And I'm sure this isn't 100 percent, all the time. However, it's a really great baseline to observe.

This doesn't mean that you want to run off and go find that mama's boy. That's a whole different ballgame. Those guys put their mother's thoughts, feelings, and opinions far above their partner's and, often, their own. That never works out well. So there are degrees. But having a man who can treat his mom with respect, kindness, and thoughtfulness will likely transcend all relationships with women. This innate behavior signals that there is an appreciation for all women.

Another suggestion that I heard over and over from men and women alike was "not on the first date." (Yep, I am talking about sex.) We've all been there ... That first-date romance is all around us. We're dressed up, looking sharp. The lighting is good. Not to mention we've probably had a couple drinks, so we're feeling happy. Oxytocin (the love chemical we naturally create in our bodies) is being produced. We are doing the flirt dance and really connecting. It's natural to want to be physical. But is it smart? Nope.

You don't know a darn thing about this new guy or gal. You're working off surface stuff. You haven't found out about the deep, meaningful issues that everyone has and lugs around beneath the surface. Not to mention the health concerns. I don't know if you've heard, but you can't tell if someone has a sexually transmitted disease by just lookin' at 'em. Needless to say, it's normal to want to hop between the sheets if it's a really great first date. Just don't. Leave something for later.

It's hard to believe that our parents may actually have some insight that is still relevant to us. As old and outdated as they may seem, wisdom is wisdom, in dating and in life.

Twenty-Seven

Take Your Own Advice

Do as I say and not as I do. Isn't that the best saying? We know that we give good, strong, rational advice to others. But, man. Taking our own medicine is really difficult. We can have the best perspective on everyone else's issues, but when it comes to our own stuff, we are our own worst enemies. Even when we get a consensus, allowing multiple sources of advice into our world, we still plow forward believing what we want and acting as we choose. And how many times do we come to regret that decision that we made in haste or under duress? So, let's learn to take our own advice.

Clients often come to me with financial issues. Time and time again, I have told them to not spend beyond their means, don't let credit card debt pile up, and be financially responsible. While I was dispensing this sage advice, I was not following by it. Hypocrisy! My boyfriend had a substantial credit card debt, which I was partially responsible for. Did I follow my own advice? No. If he could ignore the calls and bills rolling in, I could too. It got to the point where we broke up; he took the furniture and my good credit with him. I was left with no couch, no TV, and no money. I had to buy paper plates and lawn chairs and start to rebuild my credit and financial responsibility. If I had listened to my own advice, I would have saved myself a whole lot of heartache and credit issues, but thankfully that is in the past and all resolved. I learned from it, albeit painfully.

Be patient. Remember how our parents drilled this into our psyche as a child? Speaking for me, personally, it's still something I struggle with, regardless of my mom's diligent efforts. Nothing can benefit a relationship more than embracing a little bit of patience. Patience calms not only our emotions but, also, our minds to make better decisions and, ultimately, convey our ideas in a more concise manner. Not to mention, in those moments of conflict or tension, it gives the opposing party (your loved one), by your pause, time to rethink their own actions. It's a win-win, and it's free. Maybe the old saying should be "An ounce of patience (instead of caution) is worth a pound of cure."

I've seen this saying in countless women's boutiques, read it on many kitschy plaques and heard it in almost every chick flick known… "No boy (or girl) is worth crying over." And if they are, they won't make you cry. Now, does this mean we should really, truly buy into this when it comes to a long-term, committed relationship? No. Life happens and brings trials and tribulations. However, I do buy into that thought when at the onset of a new relationship. Anyone worth any time and effort shouldn't bring you to tears early on. That's the time for the fun and excitement. The beginning of the relationship is meant to plant the seeds of greatness that gives you a foundation for potential harder times (and those, my dear, may make you cry). Relationships should start with laughter, exploration, and good times—not tears. If sadness and heartache are the early basis for the relationship, move on. You can't expect to benefit from something that starts badly.

How many thousands of times have we suggested that a friend, family member, or partner just *relax*. Take a breath. It's good advice. When we take a deep breath, by simple biology we are able to calm ourselves down, but on another note I would not recommend anyone to tell another to calm down. Always seems a little demeaning or condescending. It's inevitable. We'll get upset over something said or done by our loved one. We're all human. Before we explode and retaliate, take a moment and really try to relax. As angry as we all get, the moment that we can temper our temper (how's that for a play on words?), we can move forward from the anger and conflict. The fact of the matter is this: when we get angry, emotions rule our communication. However, that same temper blocks external communication from being fully understood. All of us have, in a moment of extreme hurt, failed to listen to anyone, regardless of the softening words being conveyed. We're not in a place to listen; hence, we only take in partial words or thoughts. The moment we relax, we become better listeners and communicators.

This brings me to my next point… Listen twice as much as you talk. There's a groovy saying about God giving us two ears and one mouth to listen twice as much as we speak. Good stuff to be certain. We all get caught up with the inner dialogue that continuously runs through our head. Unfortunately, when we get upset, that inner dialogue becomes much louder than what is being communicated to us externally. So, really make an effort to listen rather than just hearing what is being said. Take into account not only the words, but the meaning, tonality, and emotion behind them. We'd expect no less from anyone else.

On the tails of becoming hurt and irate comes reaction. Reaction has a place in the world. If someone is bleeding and injured, our instincts take over and we react to the wound. If someone surprises us with a gift, a joyful, happy reaction is a good thing. However, reaction in relationships, when upset, isn't terribly beneficial. It's human nature, when hurt, to lash out either emotionally or physically and to protect or defend. Although it's human nature, it doesn't mean it's the evolved thing to do. I can't say this enough: stop reacting when overly emotional. Although it's instinctual, it really isn't going to get you far. In fact, it may set you back by you saying something that is completely untrue or out of bounds. Words, as we all know, can wound deeply. Be cautious with them when feeling overwhelmed. Remember this, as I've been told this by Spirit in countless readings... When we react in anger and haste, it is our ego—and only our ego—that is communicating.

If need be, seek counseling. There isn't anything wrong with seeking a little professional help. Unfortunately, the perception of some is that seeking therapy is a weakness. It's not. In my opinion, it's completely the opposite. Someone who can stand in their own issues, see them for what they are, and then ask for help is someone who has courage. Whether you feel most comfortable with a licensed therapist (psychologist or psychiatrist) or your church pastor is irrelevant. Getting an external opinion not only can be great validation but an invaluable resource. They're going to see the nuance in your behaviors and provide tools to overcome issues. Even if the final solution is to move on from the relationship, you can assuredly know that you have extinguished all options. I myself have greatly benefited from therapy (both marital therapy and just plain life). Being that Bobby and I eloped after four months of dating brought forth a lot of unique issues and quirks that still come up twenty years later. If we hadn't headed to therapy so early into our relationship, we may not have made it. We set the precedent early on that this is what we were willing to do to make it work. Divorce was not an option for getting out of this marriage. It was therapy or death.

Now let's talk a bit about what we can do to prevent ickiness from entering the relationship in the first place. For you guys out there, us girls have given these tips to our sisters for years. But it works for you, too!

Take care of yourself. How's that for being blunt? It's far too easy to get comfortable in a relationship and not feel that we have to doll up for our partner. Why should we not continue to court each other visually after the relationship is established? Let's face it. We're typically attracted to one another physically at first. That doesn't mean that that outward appearance should fade! Although, ultimately, we create a relationship with the person that is on the inside, we reflect that love externally by looking good on the outside. Now, we don't have to stroll around in tuxedos and formal gowns each and every day. That'd just be silly, and uncomfortable. But why not make sure to put on a little lipgloss or cologne when you know your partner is coming home? Heck, you probably have it lying around anyway. It just takes a little effort.

This next issue seems so simple, but I can't stress this one enough. Personal time is infinitely important. I get it. We find ourselves in a new relationship and all we want to do is spend every minute of free time with the new love. Gag, right? It's totally normal. The new relationship is exciting and all full of spark and wonder. But it's during this time that you need to still hold on to your own individualism and personality. Keep some time for yourself, outside of work. Absence does make the heart grow fonder. And who doesn't need a few extra moments to get things done for you? Whether it's going out with friends, doing the laundry, or taking some time out of the relationship to spend time with family, it will only serve to strengthen the bond between you and your new interest.

Another little tidbit... Don't force someone to fit. If it's not working for you, it's not working for you. Just because you want to be in relationship and you meet another guy/gal that's single, doesn't make them the One. Sometimes, when we feel like we are at the end of our dating rope, we just look past those irksome qualities because we want to be in a relationship. Letting things go is great for a friendship, but if there are character flaws that trouble you in the beginning of a romance, chances are they'll become bigger issues the longer you let the romantic side of things progress.

On that note, make sure to date outside your comfort zone. We all have a type. Whether it's a physical preference or something more character driven, we really do have things we are drawn to. However, just because someone doesn't look/seem right immediately, doesn't mean you should rule them out. Case in point: blind dates. My suggestion is to just go on them, 100 percent of the time. What do you have to lose? Worst-case scenario is you are out a little bit of time but have a fabulous story to share with friends and family. You may find the love of your life in the exact opposite package you had imagined. Nothing ventured, nothing gained!

This is especially for the boys... Be romantic. I hate to be a little gender-biased here, but I tell it like it is. Romance will get you far, and I don't mean any underlying message with that statement. Romance is integral to a relationship. It tells your partner that you still love and care about them in the same way you did when you initially met. That's it. It's the external way of showing the care that you have for one another. There's no need for showy or pricey gifts (although they're appreciated). That's not what romance is about. A handwritten note can be the most romantic thing in the world. Picking a flower (and yes, dandelions count) along a walk and giving it to your partner can be a cherished memory. Taking that one second and making it a moment will get you through some tough times in the future.

Twenty-Eight

Do You Need a Psychic or Common Sense?

I get it. We all want insight and tools to grow. Not to mention, we seek the all-important truth in different situations. And that's where I come in. Good people from all around the world (God bless the Internet) seek me out and ask my counsel. I'm eternally grateful. No question that I'm blessed to be able to do what I do. It's my passion. But, sometimes these lovely folks just don't need a psychic, they just need a good dose of common sense, which is what I like to call a verbal bitch-slap. And I'm happy to provide that too.

First, psychics aren't therapists. However, I've been told by many that their therapist wasn't able to get them in, so they came to me. I always thought that was kind of cute.

And a little insulting to their counselor, but I'm thrilled to be of service however I can. But let's get it straight, I don't have years of education and study devoted to understanding the human mind. All I can do is be my psychic self and pull through information and share it with my clients. I am not equipped for several years of conscientious scrutiny of all aspects of anyone's life. I get what I get and hope that my client makes the most of the information. That is all. I want to empower my clients to make the changes that they need to make in their life and let them move forward.

It's difficult to be 100 percent objective in one's own life. I get that. However, the biggest thing, before booking a reading with any psychic over an issue, is to take a moment and ask if you're just being hyperemotional. If you are, step back, gain perspective, and reason things through with logic. And don't tell me you can't. You can. Just do the "If I was giving advice to a friend, what would I tell them?" thing. It works. The hiccup is not typically that you can't be objective; it is that you don't want to face what you probably already know.

To drive home the point, I would like to share a couple stories with you. Hopefully you'll get more than a laugh out of them. These two contrasting stories clearly illustrate why sometimes you should consult a psychic, and why sometimes you just need a dose of common sense. Before you ask, yes, these stories are true.

I cannot tell you how often I hear the story from some poor, unsuspecting gal who has found the opened box of condoms. Whether they are found in a vehicle, dresser drawer, or closet, it doesn't matter. Of course, the story always goes that upon further inspection, some are missing from the package. When the boyfriend, husband, or partner is questioned, of course they are not his. The excuses are endless. A friend left them. A co-worker asked him to hold on to them. He has no idea where they came from. Or one of my favorites: it's the gal's fault for snooping around and finding them. Ladies, regardless of the circumstances, don't be fooled in this scenario, and do not call a psychic and ask, "Do you think he is cheating on me?" Just use common sense—the answer is obviously a big, fat, resounding, "Yes, he is cheating on you." Now go do something about it.

My second story is a bit strange, a little spooky, and one of the more interesting reasons ever why consulting a psychic ended up being a very good idea. A client I will call Mary came to me suspecting that her husband (I'll call him Mike) may be cheating on her. She, of course, requested that I either validate her suspicions or help her deal with the trust issues she was battling in her marriage. When I provided the reading for her I was able to see her husband Mike. However, he was cloaked in hazy fog. I was unable to see if he was alone or with another woman, but it was evident he was hiding something. I was not able to confirm or deny Mary's suspicions of cheating during this reading. However, one week later a woman I will call Sandy came to me for a reading. She had heard the story about Mary's session I had given a week earlier and was intrigued in having a reading of her own. She initially told me she was a just co-worker of Mary's, but I sensed something a little different. When I began the session for Sandy I almost immediately had to stop. What I saw forced me to ask Sandy why she really came to see me. Sandy in turn asked me what kind of question is that, and became visibly flustered. I simply told Sandy I could see what she was hiding and asked her if she wished to continue. Sandy then spilled the beans. She was Wiccan, a religion that believes in part that within nature, supernatural powers exist. Oh, it gets better. She also admitted to being the one who had covered Mike in a protective energy in order to help keep their affair a secret. She was the mistress, and Mike had been cheating on Mary all along. Needless to say, Sandy did not stick around to finish her session; she stood up, shook my hand, thanked me, and with a smile said, "I guess your psychic powers are stronger than my spells." Mike was actually the one who sent her to me after his wife Mary had told him about her reading. I could never tell Mary what I had learned; it would have been unethical to reveal details of the session I had with Sandy. I heard later in that same year that Mike and Mary ended up getting a divorce.

Conclusion

Hopefully this collection of stories, thoughts, and advice has given you some new ideas about romantic relationships. When to get out, when to make a change, what to do in certain situations? I can only pass along the information. It is up to you to put it into play. What I can promise is that contemplating the experience of my clients and myself personally will create a better prepared, more understood person. This can only lead to a more understanding individual. And understanding people make great partners.

For the guys, my husband once told me that boys would rather be punched in the face than talk about relationship stuff with another dude. To you, I hope that I was the friend, the girlfriend that gave you some sort of insight if you didn't feel comfortable talking to your guy friends. For those guys who do talk with your bros about relationship stuff...shoot me an email. I always like to contradict my husband. *giggles*

I cannot stress enough, no matter what I may have suggested earlier... Be yourself. That is always the best solution. But be the best you that you can be. Don't look to find fault, error, mistrust, or any other red flags. I think that is where a lot of us go wrong. Sometimes, when it's really right, things are just that good. Don't search for problems because the only thing you'll do is find them. You have to be true to yourself, your thoughts, your beliefs, and your ideas. No matter what, remember them and don't let them become secondary. Although you may be the most beautiful person in the world, we fall in love between the ears (brain), not with the eyes.

Live and love by the same set of rules because having two separate ways may only end up in conflict with your partner. You can have a certain expectation for your love, but not be willing to live by it yourself. Consistency in relationships is the key. If you find that you are making exceptions because it's easier for you, you're going to find you're confusing your partner and therein will lay a conflict. If you make a relationship rule, you both need to live by it. And if you make an exception, that needs to be understood in advance—well before the action needing the exception takes place.

My last little nugget of relationship advice: Be in the relationship for right now. When we meet and fall in love with someone it's all we can do to think of forever.

Of course, at that moment it's all hearts, glitter, and fluffy bunnies (at least for girls...for boys it may be fast cars, fried foods, and beer...I don't know what boys represent as love). My mantra is this: Although I want to be with my husband forever, I'm going to work on myself and my relationship from moment to moment. Forever can be pretty daunting. Stay current. If we get too focused on the forever, we really can slack off in the present, thinking that at some point, we'll rectify today's missteps. Personally, I think that's a grand mistake.

So that's it. Again, I wish that this is a work of help, comfort, and assistance when needed for everyone. Hopefully it makes you laugh. And, it's okay if some parts made you get a little teary. It's all part of the greatest gift of life: Love.

Acknowledgments

This book came about through thousands of psychic and tarot card readings I have done for people all over the world in the last couple of decades. My personal experiences in various relationships, and most of all my twenty-year-long marriage contributed a great deal of material to write about.

The stories, guidance, advice, and lessons learned contained in this text hopefully give you clarity and confidence in your own relationships.

I wish to express my sincerest gratitude for all those who contributed, knowingly or unknowingly, to this book. Additionally, I would not have been able to complete this second addition without the medical team who saved my life on two separate occasions and worked with me daily since my stroke back on January 18, 2013—words cannot express how deep my appreciation is for these gifted and skilled people, I would not be here today without them.

My heartfelt gratitude goes out to some very special people in my life who kept my spirits held high and have showered me with love and support. Although I cannot name them all here, there are a few who deserve to be distinguished. God bless Kelley and Brett F., Caitlin H., Marlene D. and her therapy dog Ella, Cathy and Kevin V., Amy G., Brian B., Stacy W., Dr. Scherr, Dr. Surri, Dr. Johnson, Heather S., Coco L., Heather K., Mike and Jo from Geppert Holistic Healing, Mark who taught me to walk again, Amber D., Shannon S., and Justin L. Needless to say, it takes a team effort and countless hours for projects like these to happen, especially now.

About the Author

Tiffany was born with abilities as a child no one clearly understood. Visions, voices, shadows, and angels that once frightened and fascinated her became her guides and ultimately her greatest gift. Being born with the ability to communicate with those who had crossed over did not sit well with some folks in Tiffany's life, with the exception of one: her mother. Even though she didn't understand the things Tiffany was seeing and experiencing, her mom knew there was nothing wrong with her daughter, quite opposite really. Her mother could see that Tiffany was someone very special and never wavered in her support, her nurturing, and her love. With that support, Tiffany flourished and grew into a wonderful, caring, and giving young adult—a parent's dream. While just in middle school she began doing tarot card readings for her friends. This was not something that always went over so well with other parents and her teachers.

By high school, Tiffany was able to give lengthy, detailed, and extremely accurate psychic readings for people of all ages and backgrounds. By the time she had graduated, Tiffany could effortlessly tap into the other side and communicate back and forth with those who had passed over. Going off to college to study marketing, Tiffany never gave thought that her gift would actually become her career. At twenty-one, Tiffany met a boy; they fell in love and then eloped just a few months later. Bobby and Tiffany were married July 6, 1994, on a beach in Montego Bay, Jamaica. Tiffany pursued her in career in marketing, quickly moving up the ladder and finding great success with the companies she worked for. However, one day in 2000, Tiffany could no longer ignore her calling; she listened to her guides and without notice walked away from her high-paying marketing job. Bobby did not necessarily agree with this decision from a financial point of view, but much like her mother did many years earlier he supported Tiffany to follow her dreams. Without a concrete plan in place, Tiffany left her future up to her guides and within days they put her on a path that would not only change her life but the lives of all those around her—past, present, and future.

For the next couple of years Tiffany traveled an hour each way, six days a week to a metaphysical store in the riverside town of Stillwater, Minnesota, where she sat and waited for walk-in clients who were looking for tarot card and psychic readings. Word spread very quickly throughout the metaphysical and paranormal community about this young woman with uncanny abilities. Tiffany not only gave these walk-in clients incredibly accurate readings, she touched many of their souls in a very deep spiritual and life-changing way. She developed and nurtured close relationships, friendships, and even business partnerships with her clients over this period of time and to this day she remains in close contact with dozens of them. It was also during this time that Tiffany struggled to accept that her gift was becoming a business and that there were also some very nefarious people in the world who were willing to try and exploit her abilities for their own personal gain. With the help and support of her husband, friends, and various client relationships, Tiffany eventually decided to venture out on her own.

She began doing readings out of her home, launched a website, and booked herself to attend metaphysical and paranormal expos around the country. She even opened up her own office space in her hometown of Burnsville, Minnesota. In 2004, Tiffany authored her first book, *Seeds of Thought: A Comprehensive Guide to the New Age.* By this time Tiffany was an internationally known psychic, speaker, healer, and teacher. Never satisfied, Tiffany continued to grow not only her businesses but more importantly her gifts and abilities. Tiffany took numerous classes on a wide variety of subjects that included theology, crystals and stones, and even kung fu. She became a certified hypnotherapist, a Reiki master-teacher, and an ordained minister. Over the ensuing years, Tiffany would write more books, produce DVDs, meditation CDs, and healing oils, and travel nonstop around the country giving gallery and personal readings, lectures, and healing and spiritual guidance.

All was going well for Tiffany in her business, her marriage, and friendships until Friday, January 18, 2013, when God chose to put Tiffany on a whole new path in life. At just forty years old and immediately following a chiropractic adjustment on her neck, Tiffany suffered a massive stroke so severe she was given little chance to survive. A life-saving angioplasty surgery gave some hope that Tiffany would pull through this horrendous event, but she had also suffered incredible damage to her brain. Within hours that glimpse of hope turned to desperation when the surgeons informed her family that Tiffany's brain was swelling so badly it would take her life if something drastic were not attempted immediately. Tiffany had to undergo a craniotomy in order to alleviate the pressure caused by the swelling of the brain. Once back in ICU, it became a waiting game to see if Tiffany would survive, and if she did, the prognosis was grim. The doctors said it was likely she would never walk, talk, or be able to swallow again. Her husband, Bobby, remained at Tiffany's bedside, accompanied by their best friend Chris, who just nine months earlier had undergone a craniotomy after an in-line skating accident. After three-and-a-half days, at 3:30 am, out of the blue Tiffany opened her right eye, gazed at Bobby and Chris, then raised her right hand and gave the peace sign. This was a moment of realization Tiffany was still there; she recognized her loved ones and was fighting to live on. She spent the next four months in the hospital and skilled nursing recovering from her stroke, which caused entire left side paralysis, loss of vision, and a multitude of other medical problems. It took two weeks just to get Tiffany sitting upright on the side of her hospital bed and required the assistance of three medical staff—it was clearly going to be a very long and painful road to recovery. Over time, her hospital room became a very spiritual place where a series of medical miracles would occur that astounded medical staff and gave her family great joy.

Over weeks and months, Tiffany learned to speak again and even learned to walk with the help of orthotics and assistance. During her time in the hospital, there were several very special people who came into Tiffany's life. Like angels sent to watch over an angel, they spent hours, days, and weeks taking care of Tiffany in countless different ways. One of her nurses (a mother of five young children) came in on her days off and worked an incredible three-and-a-half-week stretch without a break, tending to every personal need imaginable. It was clear Tiffany would survive and live a much different life moving forward but one big question remained unanswered. Would

Tiffany still have her gift? Was she still psychic? Tiffany answered this question in her own unique and special way. One evening in the rehabilitation unit, Tiffany was eating dinner with other patients. The lady sitting next to her was struggling both emotionally and physically. Tiffany reached over, put her hand on the woman's shoulder, and whispered to her that she was going to be okay, that she would heal quickly, and actually predicted the day she would get to go home—some nurses chuckled about the release date Tiffany gave this patient. Over the next few days this patient made an incredible recovery and was discharged from the hospital on the exact day Tiffany predicted, which was an astonishing three weeks earlier than what the doctors had estimated. Over the remaining time that Tiffany spent in the hospital, she would perform numerous readings and predictions for doctors, nurses, and surgeons. Tiffany's gifts and abilities we're clearly unaffected by the stroke. Oddly enough, Tiffany may have explained this good news in a comment she had made many years earlier during an interview. Tiffany stated that she felt her abilities came from energies in her spine and never believed they came directly through the brain itself. Tiffany was cleared to go home in the spring of 2013 and to this day works relentlessly on her recovery—she remains surrounded by angels.